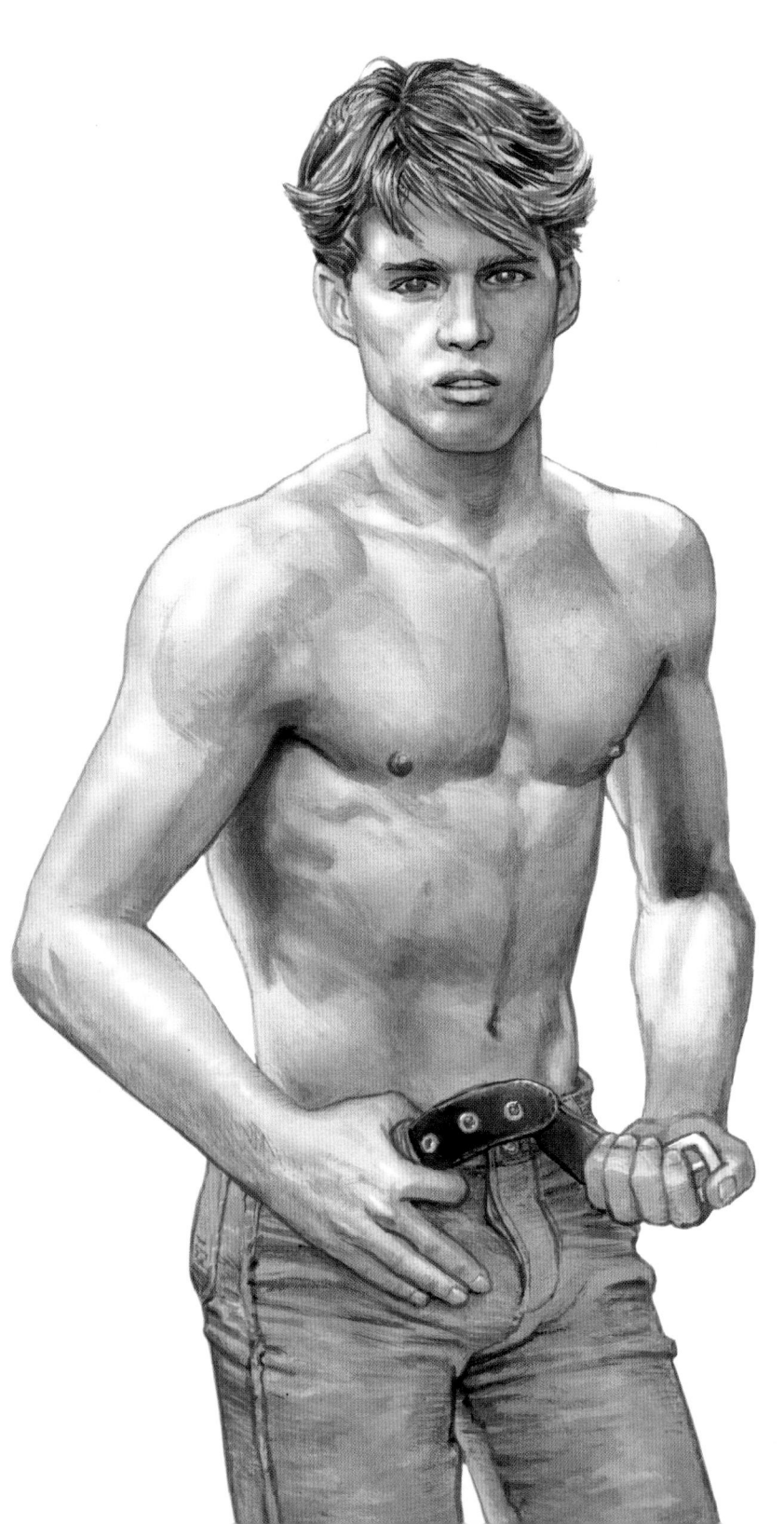

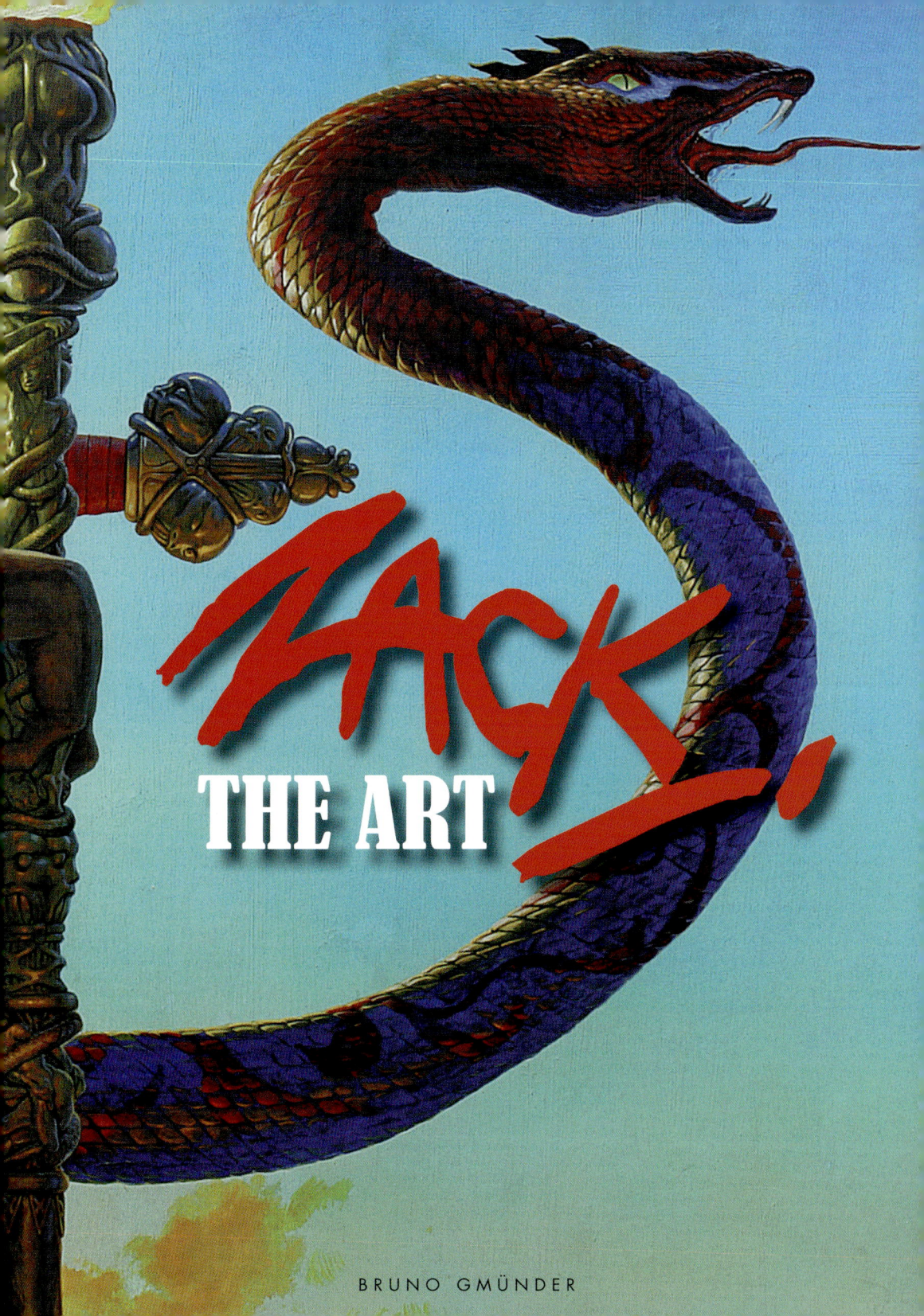

Contents

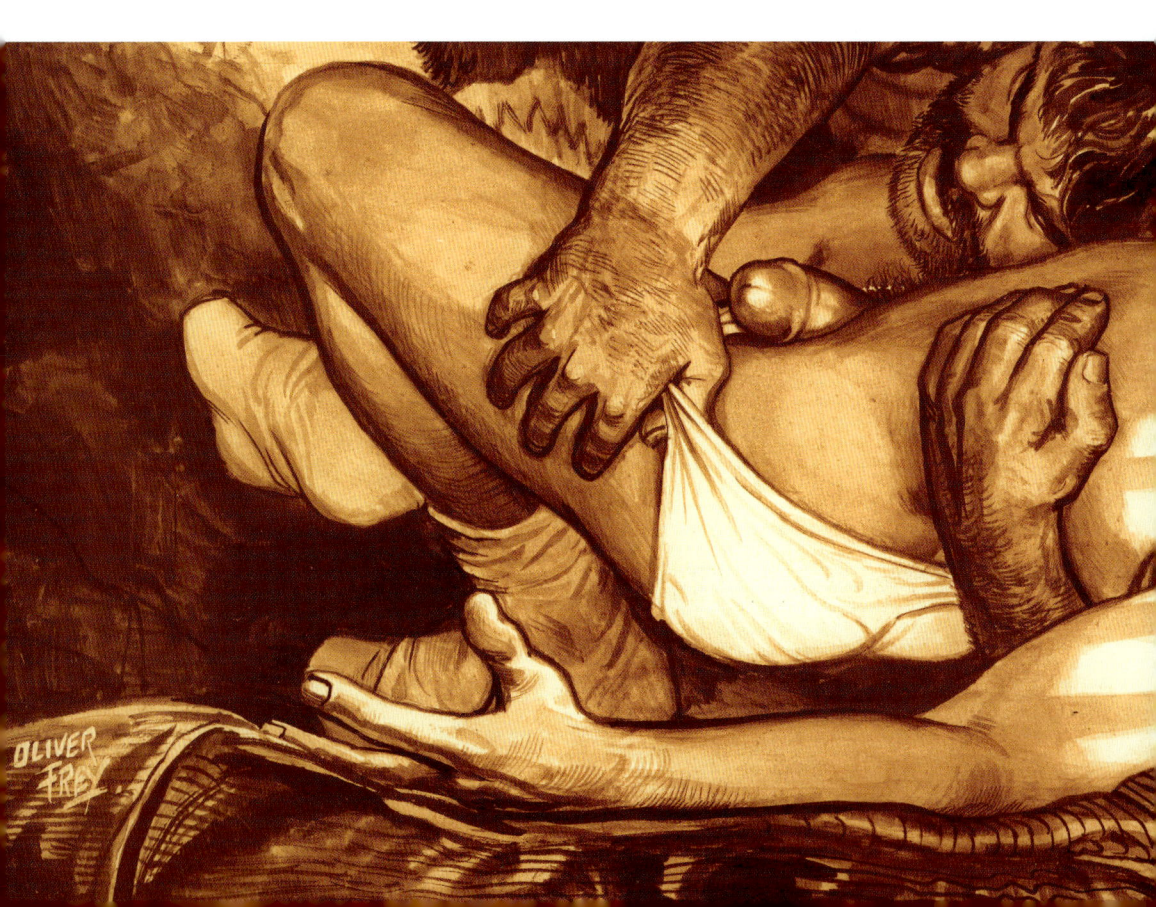

Boy Next Door 10
Boys in Love 28
Getting Wet 44
Fantasy 60
Heavy Intent 80
Full On 122
Over the Top 170
An Art Amatorius 196
Covers, Adverts, Posters 206
Afterword 234

Who can deny the allure of young males? Fresh faces, cheeky grins, surly glowers, teasy eyes, promising pouts. Innocent or knowing, their bodies sturdy or slim bring on a tingle of attraction and a promise of fun. Zack masterfully creates these boys of your fondest dreams—he knows the naughtiest imaginings can be fulfilled by that most natural of beings—the...

Boy Next Door

12	A Tasty Morsel
13	Hot Dog Boy
14	Strawberry Boy
15	Light My Fire #1
16	Light My Fire #2
17	Punk Boy
18	Sega Warrior
19	Dream Boys #2
20	Skateboarder Boy
21	Rollerskater Boy
22	Kid Hustler
22	Latino Kid
23	A Technical Hitch #2
24	The Artist
25	Valentine's Boy
26	Impact Man
27	Dream Boys #1

Boys in Love

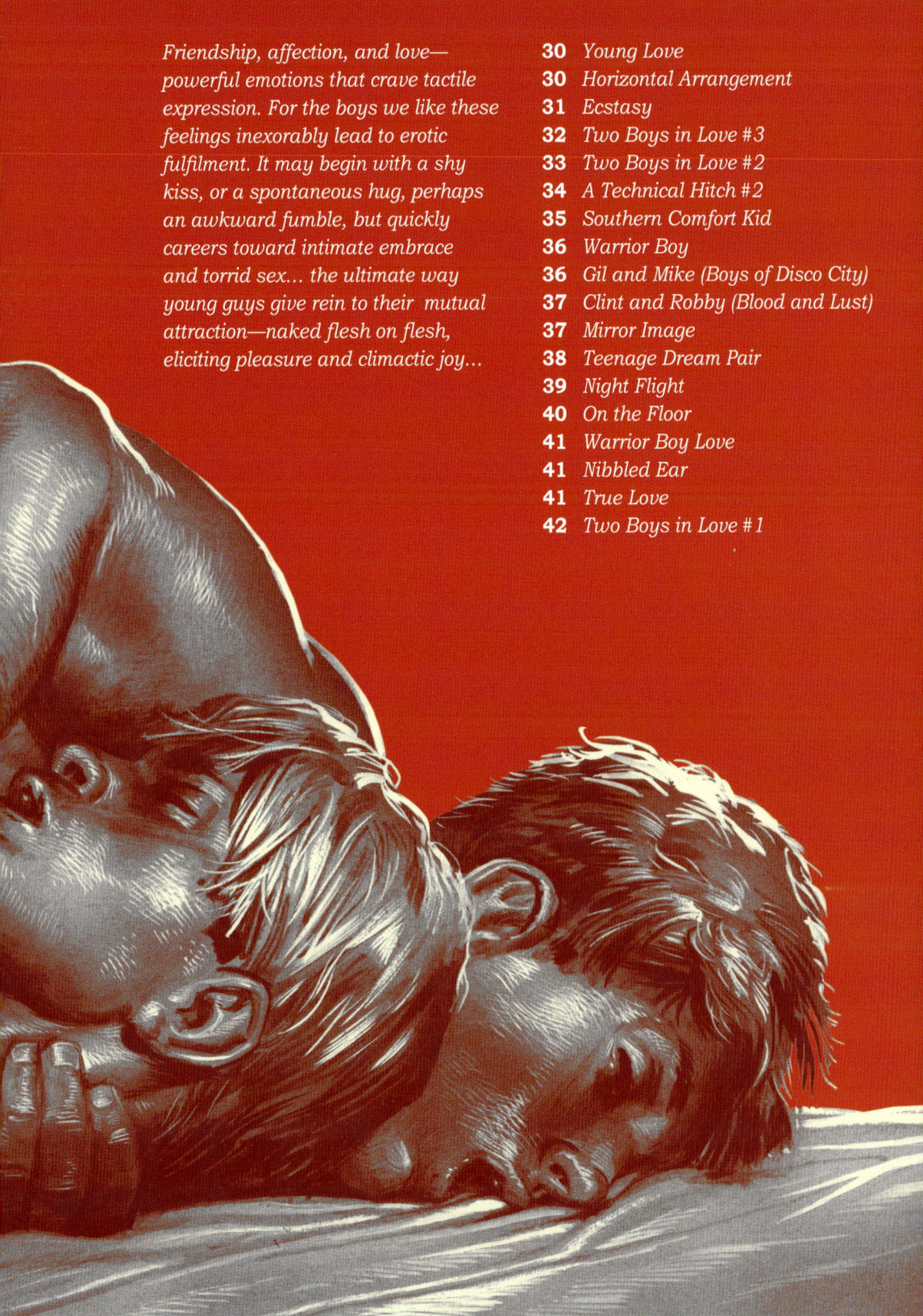

Friendship, affection, and love—powerful emotions that crave tactile expression. For the boys we like these feelings inexorably lead to erotic fulfilment. It may begin with a shy kiss, or a spontaneous hug, perhaps an awkward fumble, but quickly careers toward intimate embrace and torrid sex… the ultimate way young guys give rein to their mutual attraction—naked flesh on flesh, eliciting pleasure and climactic joy…

30 Young Love
30 Horizontal Arrangement
31 Ecstasy
32 Two Boys in Love #3
33 Two Boys in Love #2
34 A Technical Hitch #2
35 Southern Comfort Kid
36 Warrior Boy
36 Gil and Mike (Boys of Disco City)
37 Clint and Robby (Blood and Lust)
37 Mirror Image
38 Teenage Dream Pair
39 Night Flight
40 On the Floor
41 Warrior Boy Love
41 Nibbled Ear
41 True Love
42 Two Boys in Love #1

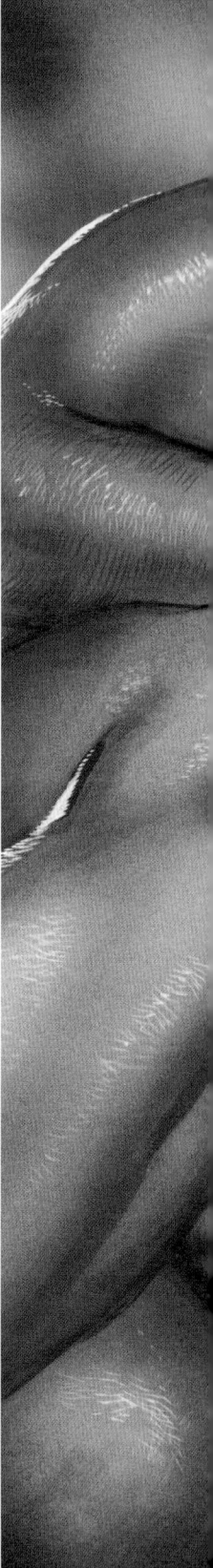

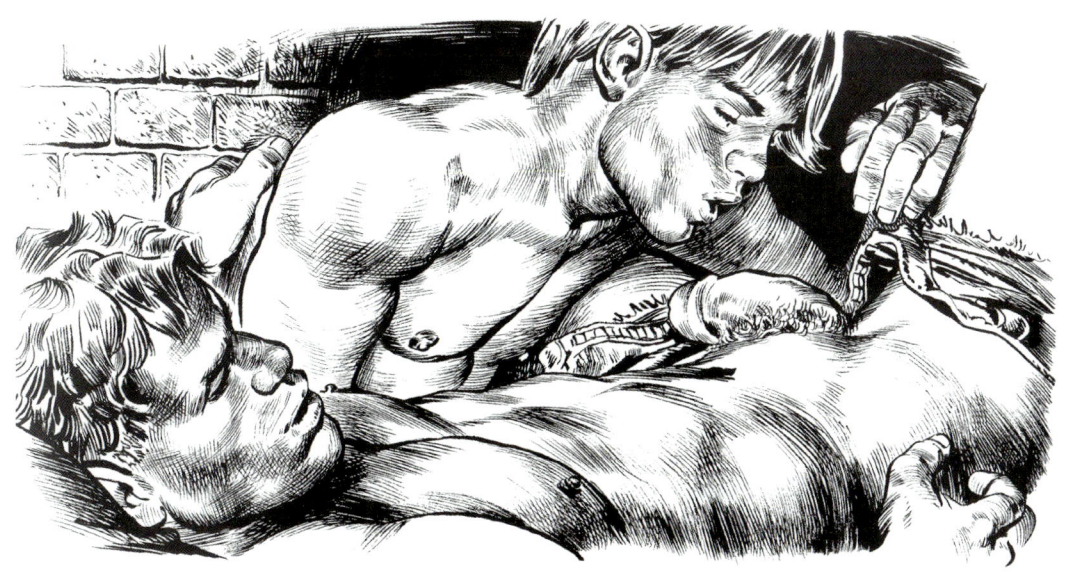

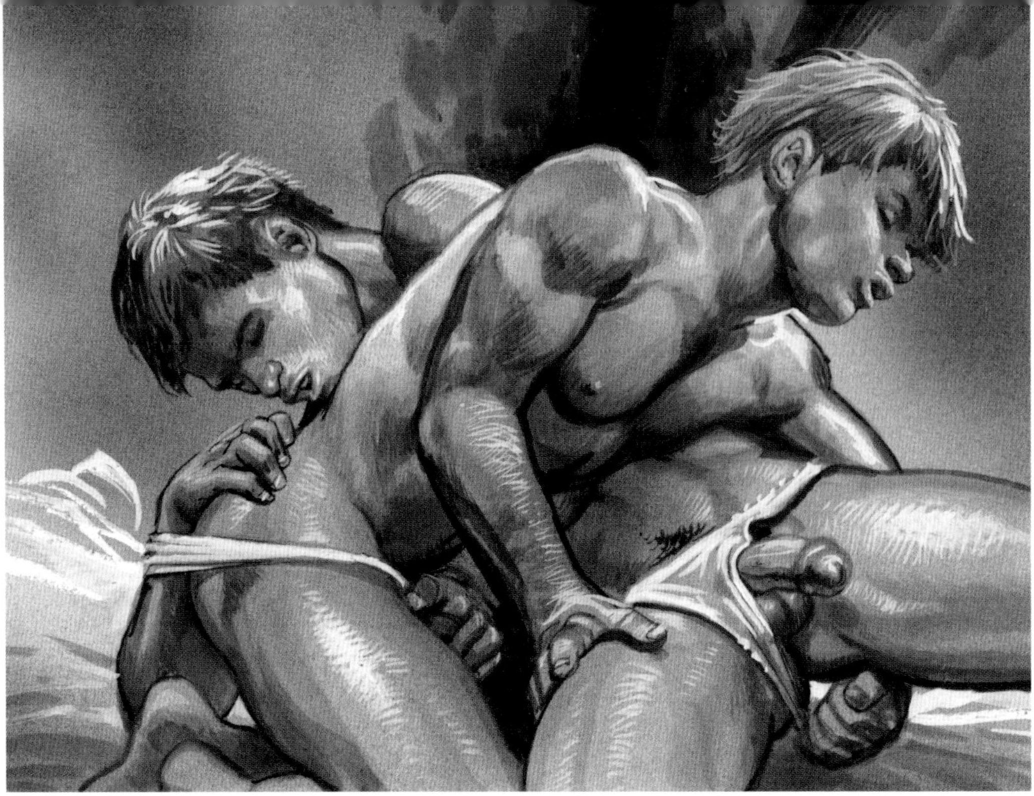

Think of water and you see moist flesh glittering with droplets, and streaked with running rivulets that accentuate every muscle and intimate fold of a guy's hot body your tongue longs to lick and taste. You see tantalizing reflections on a still surface, imagine surf breaking over passionate lovers' conjoined passions—or the always erotic notion of sex in a shower, rain-drenched fun in unlikely places. Enjoy the visual arousal of…

Getting Wet

47 *Bathing Boys*
48 *The Castaway*
49 *Warrior Boy (back cover)*
50 *Making Waves on Cebu*
52 *Locker Room Disagreement*
53 *My Name is Bond (Nightcap)*
54 *Showertime #2*
55 *Showertime #1*
56 *Acme Cleaning Company*
57 *Getting Fresh*
58 *Up Against the Wall #2*
59 *Up Against the Wall #1*

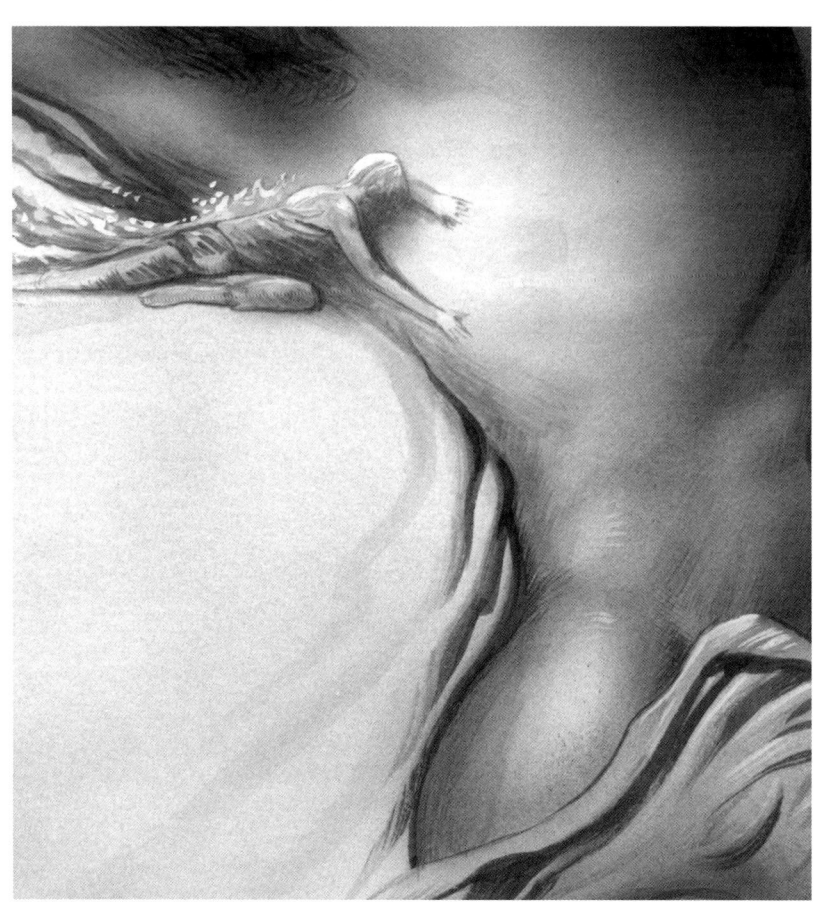

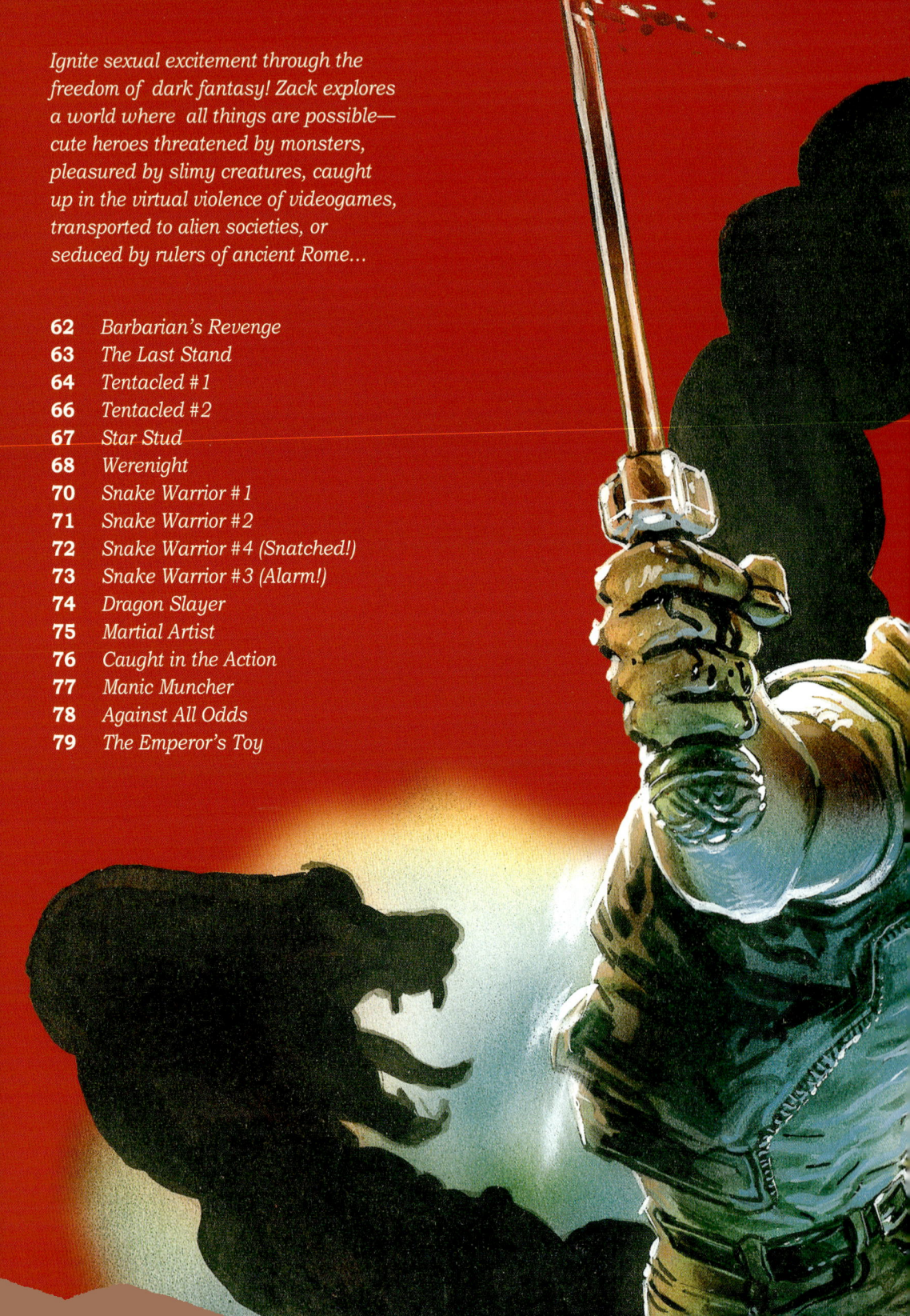

Ignite sexual excitement through the freedom of dark fantasy! Zack explores a world where all things are possible—cute heroes threatened by monsters, pleasured by slimy creatures, caught up in the virtual violence of videogames, transported to alien societies, or seduced by rulers of ancient Rome...

62	Barbarian's Revenge
63	The Last Stand
64	Tentacled #1
66	Tentacled #2
67	Star Stud
68	Werenight
70	Snake Warrior #1
71	Snake Warrior #2
72	Snake Warrior #4 (Snatched!)
73	Snake Warrior #3 (Alarm!)
74	Dragon Slayer
75	Martial Artist
76	Caught in the Action
77	Manic Muncher
78	Against All Odds
79	The Emperor's Toy

This is the point where guys stop fantasizing and make their move. They know who they want, and just how they're going to have them. Many ways lead to their goal—teasy seduction, forceful domination, or mutual lust—whatever the circumstances, Zack's boys always get their pleasure!

82 Battle Trophy
83 A Roman Spanking
84 Rogue & Young Friends
86 Love All
88 Pavilion Tea Break (Sticky Wicket)
89 Rogue Goes Rock Climbing
90 Blood and Lust
91 Park Pickup
91 Youth in the Park
92 Sweet Buns
94 Boys of Vice City
95 Scorpio Boys
96 Knickers Off
98 Life Guard
99 Bike Boy Up Against the Wall
99 Get Fucked or Die!
100 Boy Who Did It for Kicks
100 Devil's Seed (front cover)
101 Borstal Boy (front cover)
101 Danger Boy (front cover)
102 Blood and Lust (front cover)
102 Southern Comfort Kid
103 Borstal Boy (back cover)
104 Boy Who Did It for Kicks
104 Devil's Seed (back cover)
105 Danger Boy (back cover)
105 Deseet Studs (back cover)
106 On the Stairs
106 Locked and Loaded
107 Whoops-a-Daisy
108 Unwrapped
109 The Boxer
110 Long Arm of the Law
111 Pig Sticking
112 Raw Recruits
113 Samson Chained
114 Rogue centerfold poster
115 Chained to Serve
116 This Won't Hurt (Caught!)
116 For Rent
117 Caught!
118 The Rookie
119 Lubing Up #1
120 Lubing Up #2
121 Back Alley Fumble

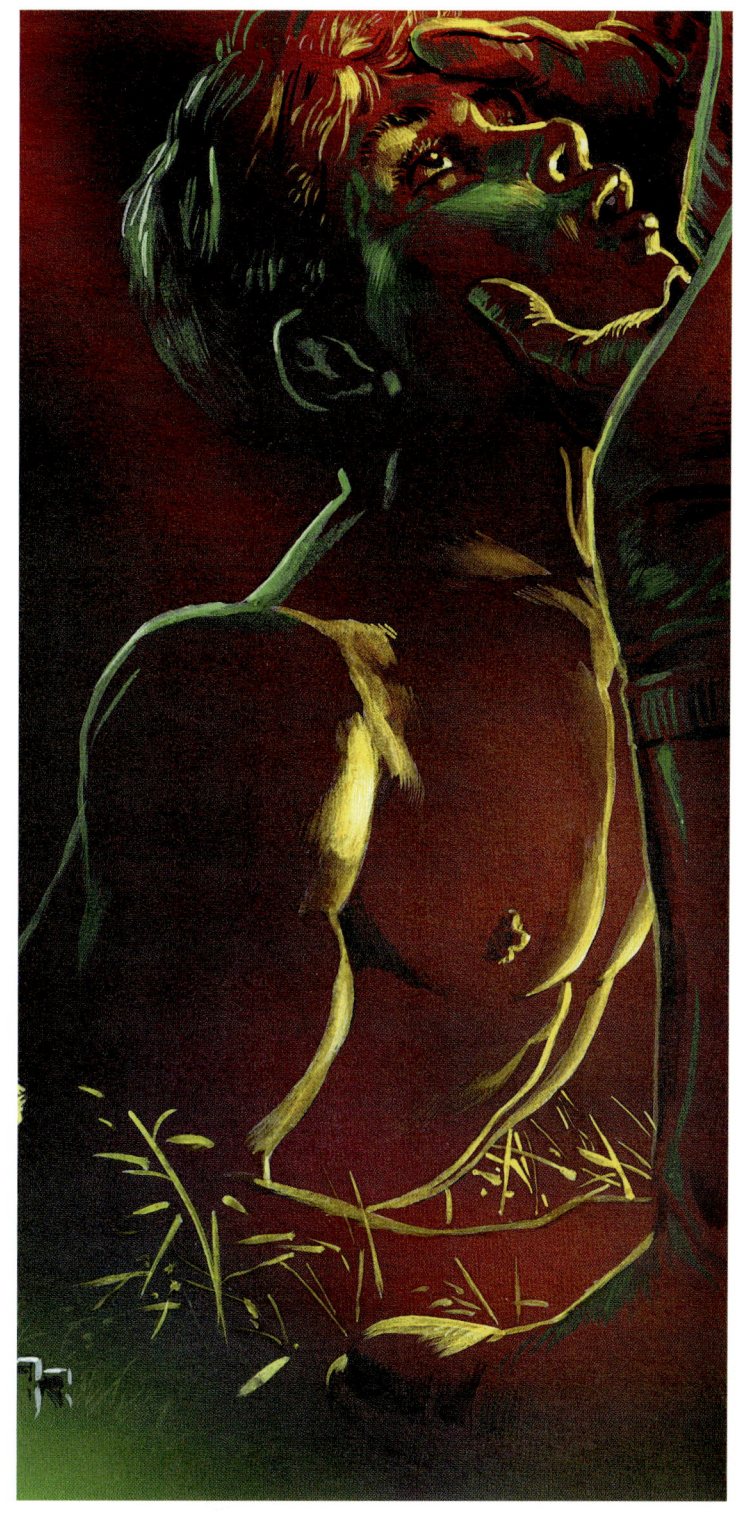

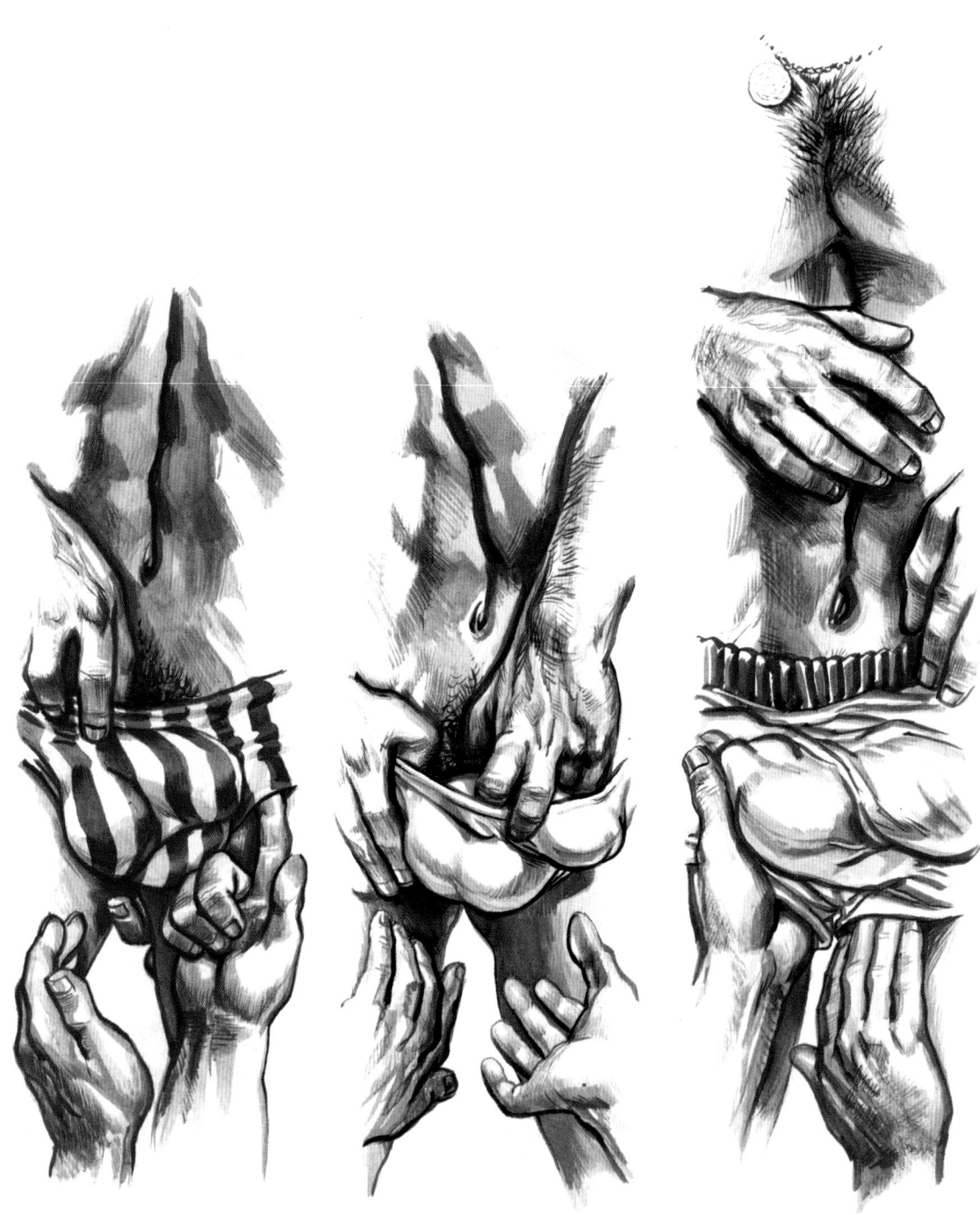

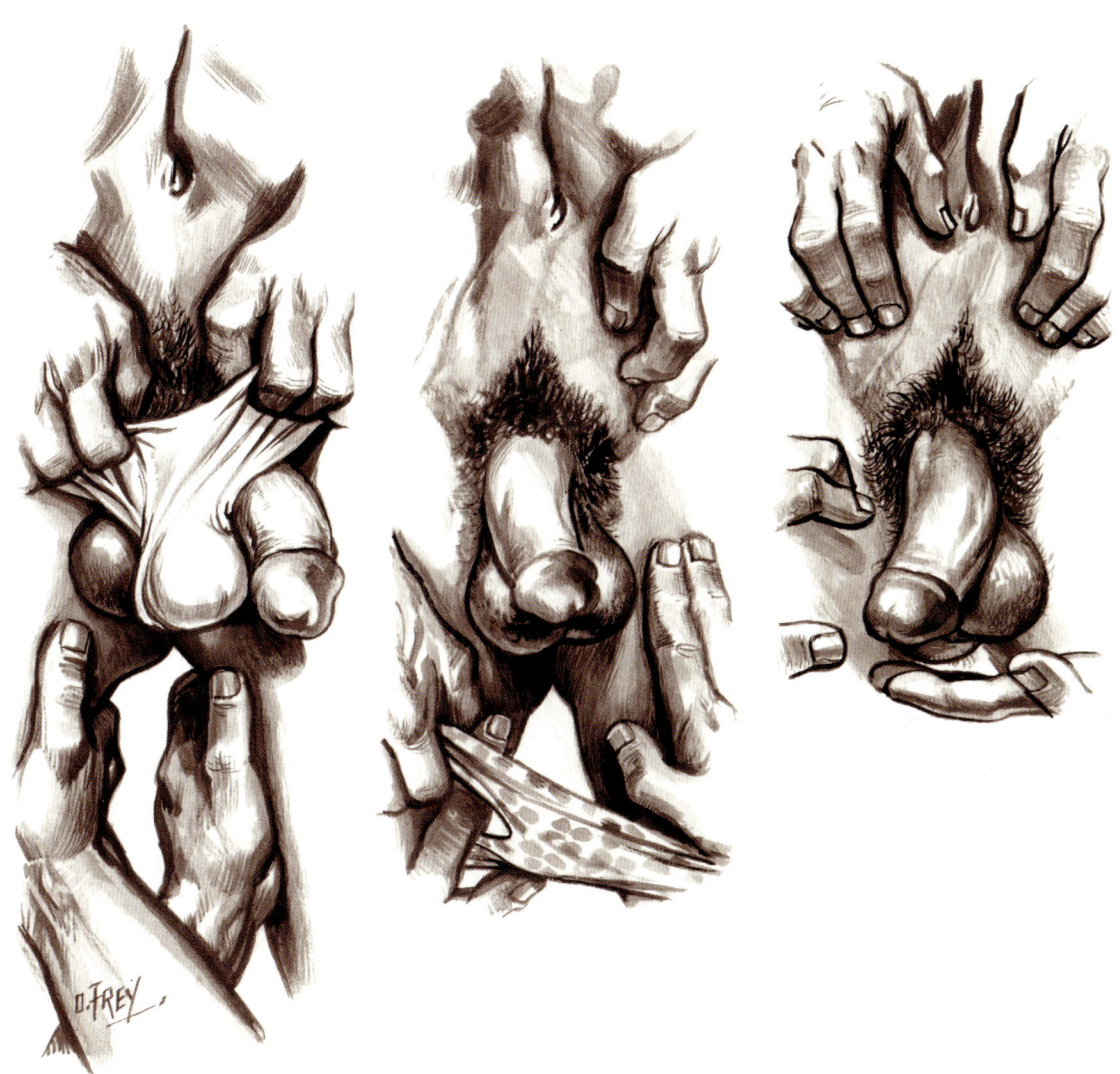

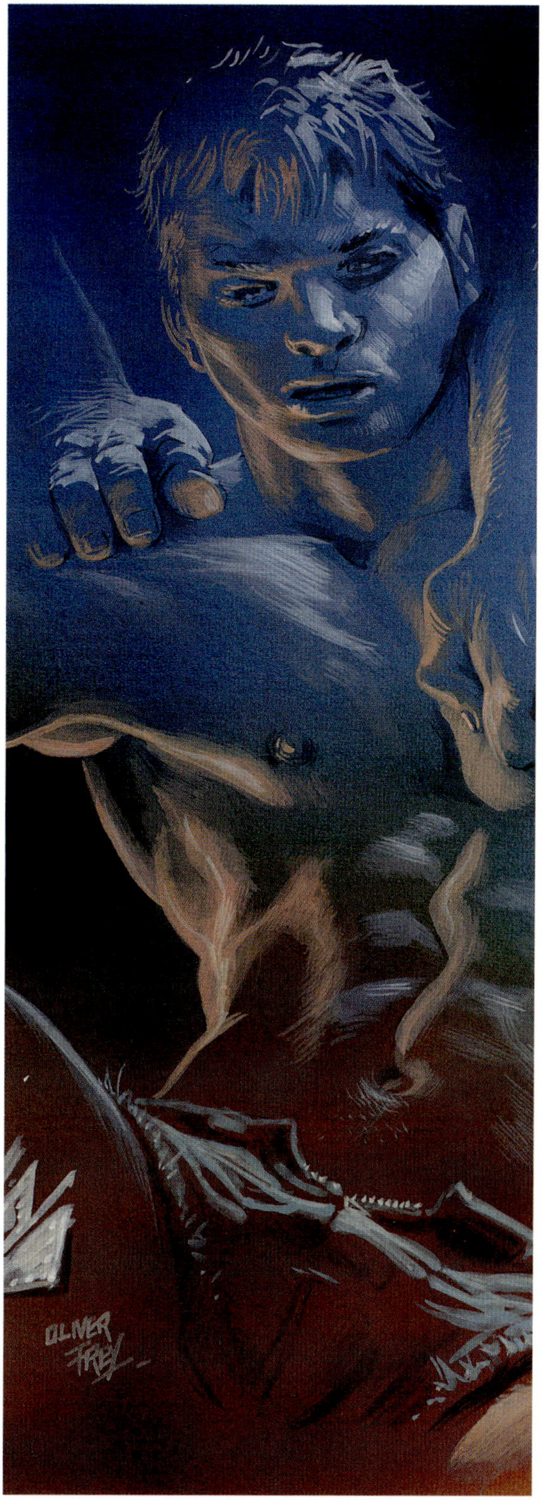

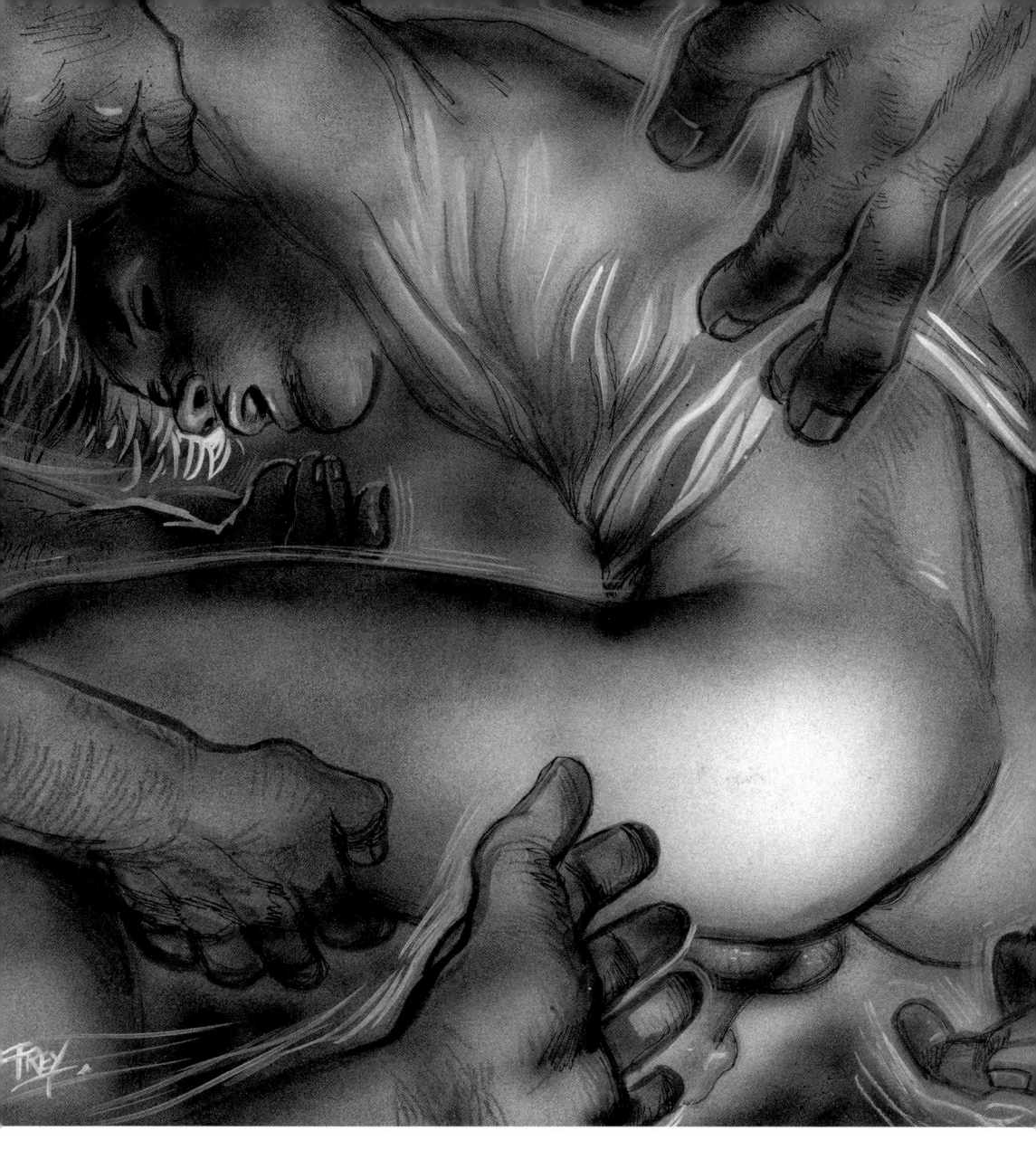

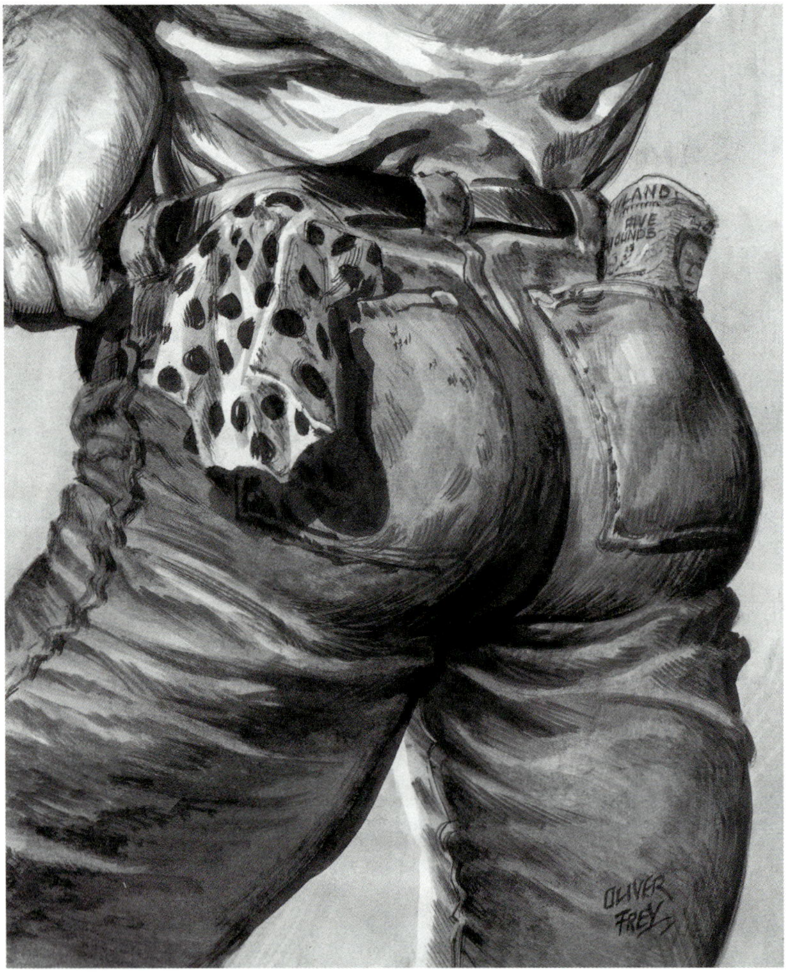

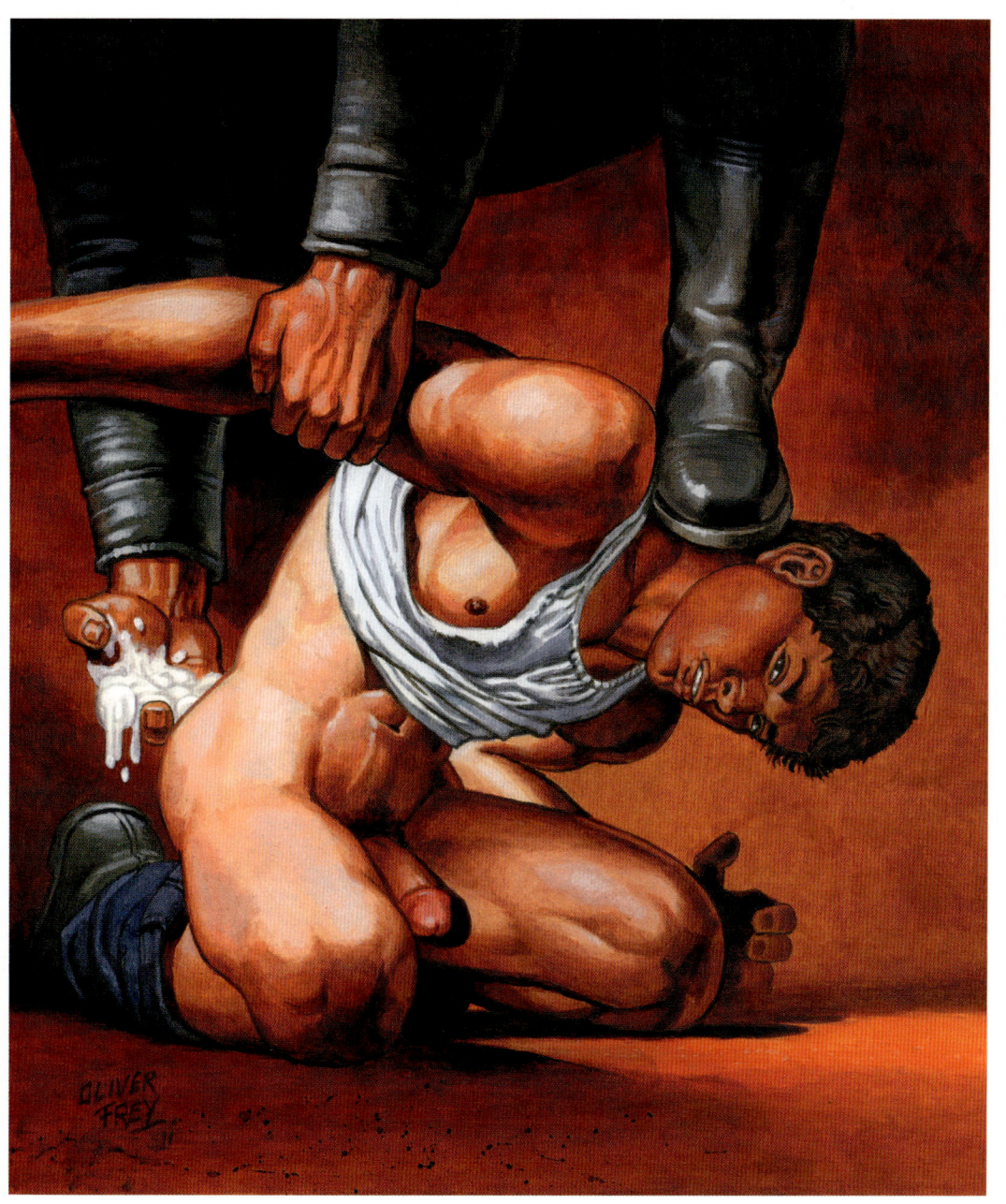

Full On

*Man on man lust unleashed!
Zack knows how to depict the visceral intensity and raw ecstasy of gay sex. Twisted limbs, grasping hands, greedy lips, contorted faces, rigid erections, and gushing orgasms evoke the pleasures we all long for. In our dreams these men and boys could be us…*

124 *The Autograph Hunter*
126 *Back Alley Encounter #1*
127 *Back Alley Encounter #3*
128 *Back Alley Encounter #2*
129 *Back Alley Sex*
130 *Devil's Seed*
131 *Battle Tank*
132 *The Hitcher*
134 *Fun on a Swing #1*
135 *Bellhop's Tip*
136 *Anyone for Dennis?*
138 *Road Warrior*
139 *Bike Boy in a Skid*
140 *High Speed Bike Action*
141 *Extra Training*
142 *Take It #1*
142 *Take It #2*
143 *Jockeying For Position*
144 *Scout's Honor*
145 *First Punter*
146 *Juicy Target*
147 *Jumberjackin'*
149 *Foreshore Play*
150 *Neck Lock*
151 *Paying For the Ride*
153 *Paper Delivery Boy*
154 *Plowing the Gardener*
155 *Prince's Pleasure*
156 *Winner Takes All*
157 *Police Procedure*
158 *Rim Nor Reason*
159 *Road Repairman's Hut*
160 *Sailors Under the Boardwalk*
161 *Vacation Break*
162 *Trucker's Rest Stop Break*
163 *Adobe Fun (Cheap Bambino)*
164 *Black on White*
166 *Tasty Morsel*
168 *The Long Lick*

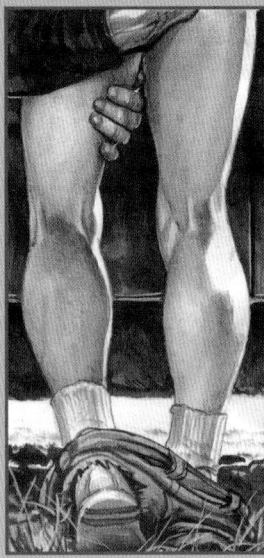

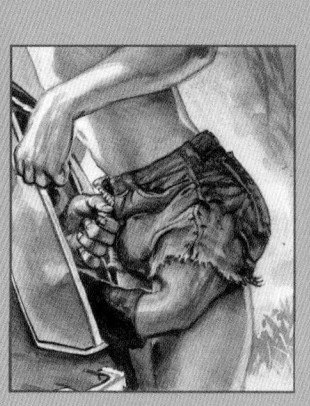

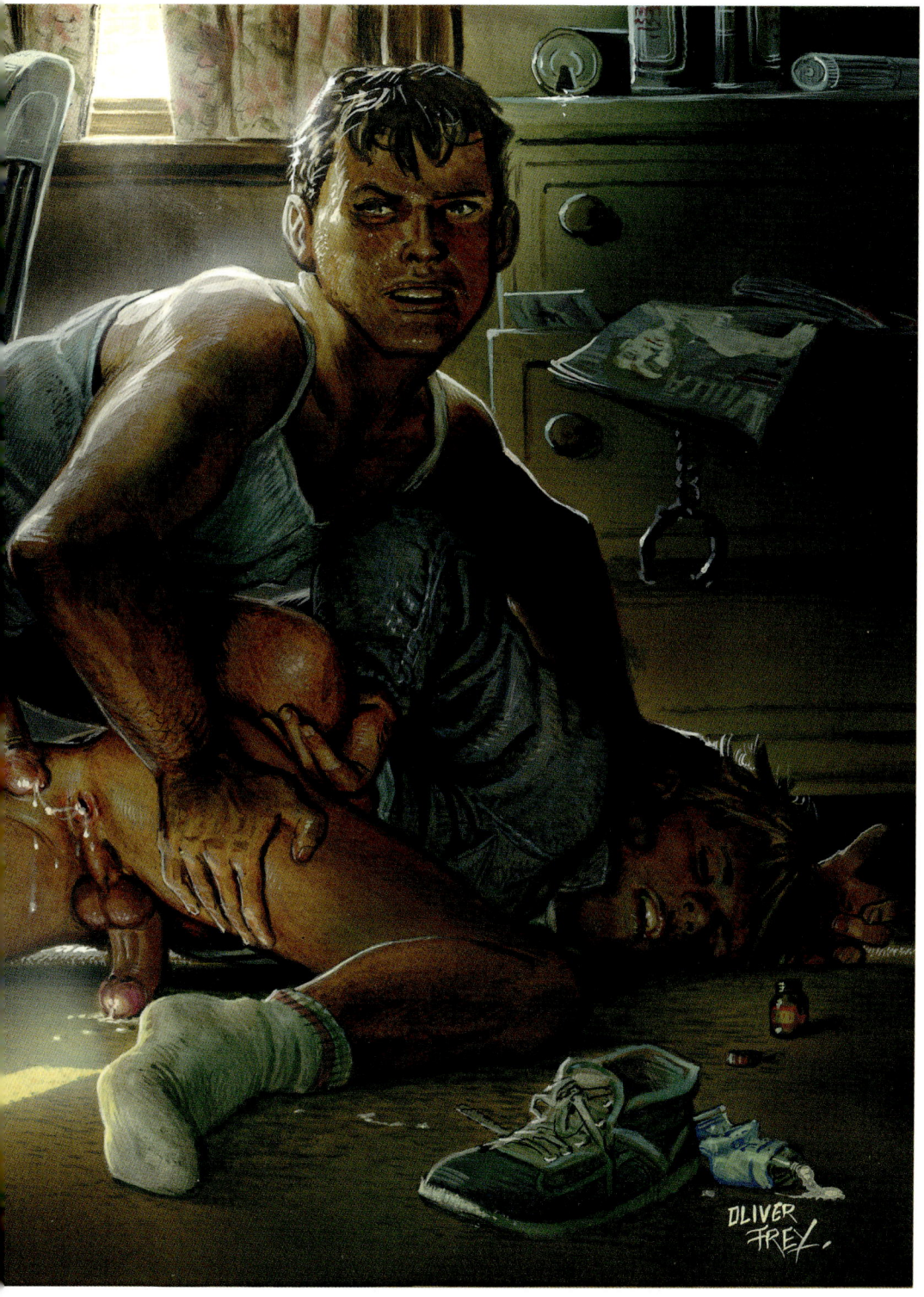

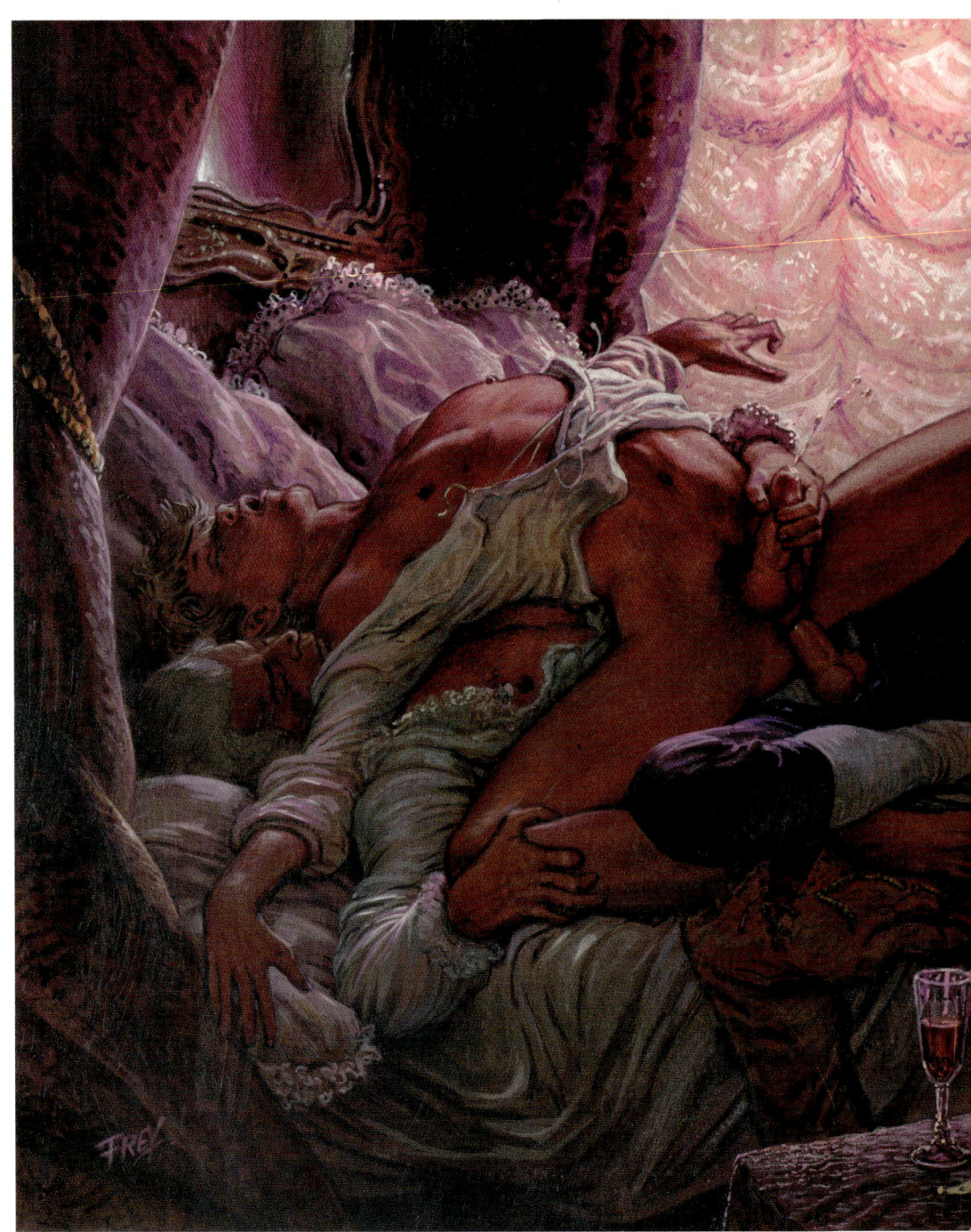

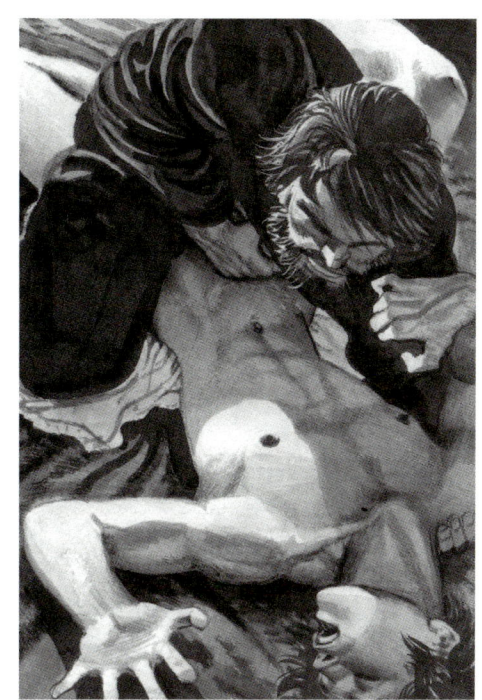

Zack's art is all about erotic fantasy, and with sex enough is never enough. Who doesn't dream of orgies where everything goes and all are willing to give and take without let-up? Well, the following images go all the way...

Over the Top

172 *Athletic Threesome #1*
173 *Athletic Threesome #2*
174 *Rough and Smooth #1*
174 *Rough and Smooth #2*
175 *Rough and Smooth #3*
175 *Rough and Smooth #4*
176 *The Erotic Dream*
178 *Rough Sex #1*
179 *Rough Sex #2*
180 *Disco Party*
181 *Roman Orgy*
183 *Giant Roman Orgy*
185 *In the Bushes*
186 *Roman Tuition*
189 *Spoils of War (Vikings)*
190 *Spoils of War (Renaissance)*
192 *Spoils of War (Ancient Greece)*
194 *Spoils of War (Huns)*

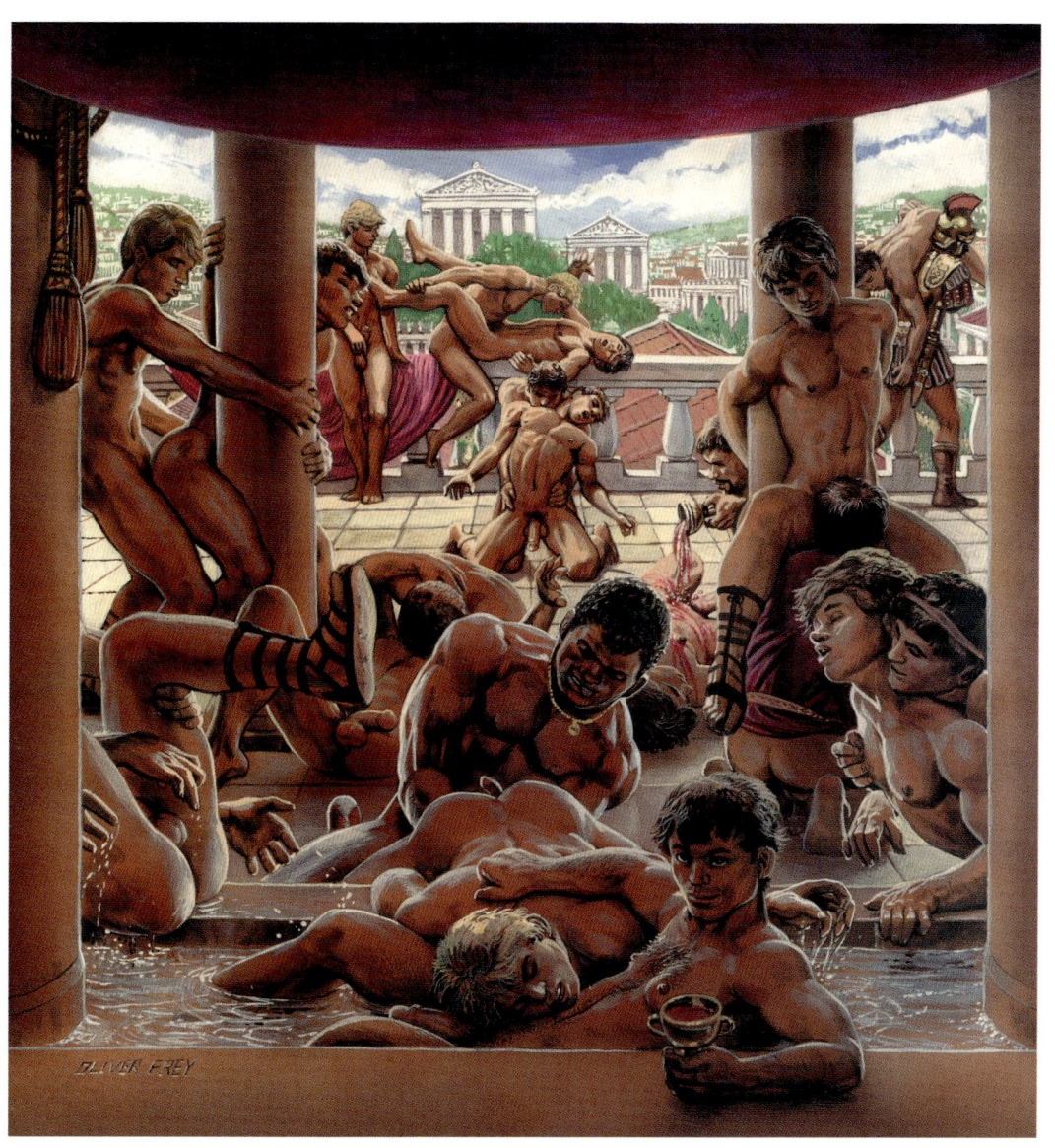

ZACK

AN ART AMATORIUS

Biography by Roger Kean

The name of Zack rings loud throughout the gay world as one of the foremost creators of erotic imagery. "This artist has divine imagination... insightful into the workings of the mind, a Da Vinci, in effect..." "Zack's stunningly erotic *Bike Boy*, which I rate the hottest piece of erotica—written, drawn, or filmed—I've ever seen." "What sets him apart from his peers is his narrative sense. The ability to tell a story is something that sets pin-up art apart from good comics art... it's beautifully rendered, erotically charged, and has a very clear, distinct narrative."

These quotes represent just a tiny fraction of the praise heaped on Zack's output over the years. But Zack (or sometimes in the past, Clint) is really Oliver Frey. As an illustrator of mainstream work, including masses of children's books, it's to be expected that he might have a pseudonym for the erotic pictures. But in fact, Zack came later in his career. At the outset of painting gay pictures, with gay liberation a new byword, Oliver Frey found the idea of signing his work with a pseudonym unacceptable. "It seemed necessary to do my bit for the gay cause as it fought for recognition during the Seventies," he has said. However, he did reconsider when, during the later 1980s, he was partly responsible for running a very straight publishing company whose output was aimed at teenaged boys, and so became briefly "Clint" for a few pictures bought by a Scandinavian publisher. Later still, while employed by a very straight-laced American publisher, "Zack" made his first appearance for the *Meatmen* comic books.

Of course, the Internet has exploded all that. Anyone can put the pieces together with a few moments on Google, so Zack remains as a useful

Above: proud mother Giulietta and baby Oliver (1948). Right: Oliver aged 11 with brother Franco below. The young Frey was beset by homoerotic urges. Far right top: Oliver in his Signal Corps Swiss Army uniform aged 18. Far right below: pictured in London while at film school, aged 21.

brand more than a pseudonym to hide behind. As at the start, Oliver Frey is out in the open again.

As the author of this brief biography, I must confess to a vested interest. I have known Oliver Frey since we met at the London Film School and have been his partner in life ever since. It means I know just about everything, but in the interests of brevity, it's been difficult to decide what to leave out, otherwise there wouldn't be any room for the pictures, which is after all the point to the book.

Early years and influences

Oliver Frey was born June 30, 1948 in Zurich, Switzerland, the eldest of three children. He grew up a fluent Italian speaker, since his parents hailed from Ticino, the southernmost Swiss canton, where Swiss-Italian is the language, but schooled in Zurich, he also learned German and French. In 1956, when he was almost eight, the family moved to Britain and the youngster discovered *Eagle* comic and the cover hero Dan Dare, Space Pilot of the Future.

When he started school in Wembley, a northern suburb of London, Frey discovered that most of his schoolmates were comics-mad, especially for *Eagle*. There had been no such comics in Switzerland, and he was taken by the quality of the artwork. Reading the weekly comic and watching television, he soon learned English, and then he started to copy the drawings of *Eagle*'s artists, and their styles became seminal influences. The feeling of bodies in movement, often in violent action, captured his imagination and is a quality that has never left his work.

Above: Roger Kean and Oliver Frey pictured on a film "recce" at Doune Castle, Scotland in 1974.
Right: contemplating a career as a gay artist in London in the mid-70s
(both paintings in oil by Roger Kean).

After a few years, the Frey family returned to Switzerland. In school, Frey had to relearn the German he'd almost forgotten. An English friend of his parents continued to send him copies of *Eagle* every week. On the due date, Frey—quite unable to wait for the postman's ring—hovered outside the front door to grab the rolled mailer. He's ever since been addicted to the post's arrival; a sense of fearing to miss out on anything, even today when most of it is junk mail. That feeling of eternal anticipation is also reflected in many of his best paintings, when the viewer senses that the artist has deliberately captured a moment just a split-second before something else interesting might happen.

The *Eagle* artists Frey most admired included the Three Franks: Frank Hampson (*Dan Dare*'s creator); Frank Humphris; and most particularly Frank Bellamy for his dramatic, action-packed line and color work. At the other end of the scale, Frey loved the work of Eugene Delacroix, again for the story-telling drama. By contrast, American comics played little part in his early artistic development. He has said that "British comics were my mainstay, followed by French comic albums. American comics that spring to mind are old Prince Valiants. The super-hero stories were too over the top for my liking."

While still at school near Zurich, Frey's attention was drawn to an advert for an

American correspondence course in illustration. The Famous Artists was expensive, but his parents paid for it, and from its invaluable lessons the young illustrator honed his skills at figure drawing and composition, both in line and in color. At the same time he press-ganged his sister and brother as actors and began making 8mm action films with a James Bond theme. The development of his own style—as he moved away from copying his comic artist heroes' pictures, owes much to the long stints of editing the films, as he discovered how arms, legs, and torsos flexed and flowed when captured in 8mm still-motion.

Approaching the age of eighteen, and with no idea that he might have a career in illustration, Frey considered further education at a film school. He rejected the respected school at Munich ("...all too serious and New Wave...") in favor of a return to London. Before any such move, however, he began his compulsory army service, which lasted for three months of basic training and then another three months' work toward becoming a corporal. With the army service under his belt, he studied at Bern University for a short period before deciding that movies were his future. He went to England and applied to the London School of Film Technique

Frey's first paid job for a gay magazine appeared in Playguy *magazine in 1975.*

(now simply the London Film School), gained a place, and started the two-year intensive course in January 1969.

While his parents paid the tuition expenses, Frey had to support himself. He looked around for freelance illustration work and found it in the Fleetway War Picture Library series of comics. The small-format, 64-page, 150-frame black and white stories of World War II, kept him busy and in funds for years. Working in a Battersea bed-sit during the evenings, between mouthfuls of Heinz West End Grill, he pencilled and inked. His association with the War Picture Library resulted in dozens of stories and covers before he stopped doing them in the late 1970s.

Throughout the 1970s, Frey established himself as a freelance comic artist. In addition to strips for Fleetway, he worked for IPC Comics' prestigious *Look & Learn*, its spin-off *Speed & Power*, painted novel book covers for the Souvenir Press, and illustrated children's books for Hamlyn, Usborne, and Oxford University Press. In 1976, Frey took over from Don Lawrence on *Look & Learn*'s celebrated color strip *The Trigan Empire*, which he painted weekly for just over a year, by which time other events began to occupy his time, more of which soon...

And what had happened to his cinematic aspirations? At the time, being an "alien," made it virtually impossible to get a Film Union ticket to work, so movies had to take a back seat. Although in 1977 his illustrative talent did get him the job of creating the comic-strip beginning of *Superman, The Movie* (1978) directed by Richard Donner and shooting at Pinewood Studios—his talent... and the active help of the union's secretary who, it turned out, was a fan of Frey's alternative illustrations, which were beginning to emerge in the fledgling gay magazine market.

Creating a Rogue

Even before the onset of adolescence, young Oliver Frey can remember semi-erotic moments when playing Cowboys and Indians with his next door neighbor of about the same age. As a young teenager, in between penning *Dan Dare*-like comic frames, he sketched illicit images of a more sexual nature, always homoerotic. The habit persisted, and there are notebooks filled with the kind of situations which later underpinned his adult work.

During the early to mid-1970s anyone wishing to purchase a gay "adult" magazine under Britain's harsh laws would have had a hard time. There were a very few such vehicles around, such as *Jeffrey*, *Just Us*, and *Line-Up*, but only sex shops sold them, and most of those had not yet recognized that there actually was a gay market. The usual outlet for gay fantasies were *Viva* and the American glossy, *Playguy*; low-key titillation for women.

At some point during 1975, now living in a nice flat in north London's Highgate, Frey got hold of a copy of *Playguy* (not to be confused with the magazine mentioned above!), published by Incognito. The same company produced a range of gay magazines for the burgeoning market: *Hung Heavy*, *Taste of Beefcake*, *Black Studs*, *HIM Exclusive*, *Leather Studs*, and *Man*. The first thing to catch Frey's eye in *Playguy* was its comic-strip. He thought it pretty poor amateurish stuff and knew he could do better. At last, some of those teenage angst-sketches and overheated imagination might be put to good use. He immediately sat down, thought up a story, produced the three-page *The Hitchhiker*, and sent it to Incognito. *Playguy*'s editor, Ian David Baker, instantly saw its worth and published the story. He commissioned a monthly series, and Oliver Frey's professional gay career was under way.

But not for long. Early in 1976 Incognito went bust and Frey never received payment for the two strips he'd produced. However, deliverance was at hand in the form of Alan Purnell, a former partner in Incognito, who had taken with him *HIM Exclusive*, and renamed it *HIM International*. Purnell wanted a tough, butch comic-strip. He wrote to Frey, enclosing a check to cover the two missing payments for *The Hitchhiker*, and invited him to discuss a new strip. And so Rogue was born, and for seven years the no-nonsense sex-machine manhandled his way monthly through endless hunky young men and more than 250 pages of erotic entanglements (→ *Rogue, pages 85, 89, 114, 204*).

Due to the nature and obscurities of Britain's Obscene Publications Act, gay publishers had to tread carefully in depictions of male anatomy, in particular penetration was to be avoided at all costs and no full erections (generally referred to as "the angle of dangle") should be shown—preferably, none at all in any state. It's due to Frey's long self-apprenticeship in action-loaded images that he managed to satisfy both the readership's sexual longing and the stupid law's strictures throughout so many comic-strips. At the same time, he drew and painted innumerable illustrations to short fiction, both in black and white and color. Before long, the growing number of gay organizations were lining up to commission Frey illustrations for their advertisements

In 1978, Frey and his boyfriend Kean joined forces with Purnell to form Street Level, which continued to publish *HIM* together with *Teenage Dreams*, *Hot Dog*, and the *HIM Gay Library* series. Street Level also became involved with

Some of the Street Level crew at London's Gay Pride, 1978, Frey (with sun shades) and Purnell on the left.

Right: an early HIM *illustration. The generally held belief in those days was that you could get away with depicting nude men as long as there was no full erection visible, what was known as the "legal angle of dangle." Frey became expert at getting an almost hard cock to point down and conform to the desired angle.*

the mammoth gay superclub Heaven, which opened its doors in December 1979, in arranging massive theme nights promoted through *HIM* magazine. In 1980 and 1981, Frey found himself in part responsible for visualizing the events and naturally creating the posters for Gym Night, Roman Night, and Jungle Party (the first two featured in this book). The club manager always had to keep a pristine copy of the large posters (→ *Posters, pages 208, 218)* for David Hockney's collection. Frey also did a promotional poster for Heaven's leather club, The Cellar (also shown, → *The Cellar, page 34)*. The Roman Night made news throughout London and caused excitement in New York for its extravagant gladiatorial fight, slave auctions, and the culminating collapse of a huge Roman temple (designed by Frey), right onto the heads of the packed crowd below.

In later years, Frey also produced several more generic poster art for Heaven, some examples shown in this book (→ *Posters, pages 210, 213, 228*).

Police from the Obscene Publications Squad marched into Street Level's premises in 1982 and seized all stock and work in progress. The matter never came to Crown Court, but the loss of so much stock and future publications wrecked the company. Purnell having left some months before, Frey and Kean sold the rights in all the titles to Millivres, publishers of *HIM*'s rival magazine, *Zipper*. It was the start of a new era. They moved from London to the small market town of Ludlow in October 1982, where for a year Frey continued producing Rogue strips for Millivres' *Mister* magazine, and created a new gay comic-strip called The Street for the re-launched (clean) *HIM* lifestyle magazine (later renamed *Gay Times*). It conatined a lot of gritty realism and Russell T. Davies has said that in his formative years Rogue and the feel of The Street not only reconciled himself to his sexual inclinations but were a part of the inspiration behind the cult TV series *Queer As Folk* (→ *The Street, pages 236-238*).

Frey ceased all work for Millivres in mid-1983 to concentrate on an entirely new venture—the creation of a computer games magazine for the Sinclair ZX-Spectrum.

To the mainstream and back

Frey's extraordinary output of work for Newsfield, the company he and Kean co-owned with his younger brother Franco, which appeared on magazine covers and internal art, is not the subject of this volume. However, some of the imagery was undoubtedly homoerotic and a few of the pictures are included here. In spite

Dreaming of becoming a gay artist, Frey in 1974 (painting by Roger Kean).

Below: Rogue's creator with a giant cut-out at London's Heaven disco.

of the inundation of illustrative work, Frey's erotic imagination would not let him rest, and he began a series of paintings and comic-strips for his own satisfaction. Freed of the earlier legal restraints involved in publishing (and in any case, Britain was lightening up on the sexual front... a bit), these were unashamedly hard-core pictures.

Newsfield was a pioneer of electronic publishing, using Apple Mac computers, and before long Frey moved from airbrush and inks on board to composing comic-strips in Photoshop, although he continued using inks and acrylics for paintings. He also insisted on pencil and ink drawing on paper for everything, only going to the Mac to scan in the line or halftone work ready for electronic coloring. Among the comics he created for his own amusement were ones which later found their way onto the Internet via the Gaytoons website: *Bike Boy*, *Tender Bait*, and *Funfair Surprise*.

In 1998, Frey approached the Californian publisher Winston Leyland with samples intended for the *Meatmen* comic books. Leyland immediately commissioned a series of stories, which included *Message to the Emperor*, *Slaves to Lust*, and *Teasy Meat*. A fourth story about Roman gladiators was half done when *Meatmen* ceased publication. These were in color but appeared as black and white renderings in *Meatmen*, but have since been published in color by Bruno Gmünder (➔ *Meatmen, pages 224-227*).

There is an interesting footnote to the *Meatmen* period, as reported by Meatcute:

"The Meatcute staff is almost ashamed to admit that none of us really paid that much attention to Frey's work when we first saw it—probably in old issues of *Meatmen*, or something. Anyhow, like a lot of drawings we just sort of flipped past it, immediately brushing it off as 'not our style.' Then years later, someone actually read one of his pieces and realized how well put together it was. Then we started noticing the volume of his work... now, we're all huge fans. It's one of those times where there should be a book dedicated to all of Frey's erotic work, or maybe one that collected his Rogue works and then one for all of the rest."

Most of Meatcute's wishes have already been fulfilled, and with this volume, hopefully all of them.

While amusing himself at weekends and evenings, between 1993 and today, Frey has worked for magazine and book publishing companies on material as varied as popular music, sports, sticker albums, and historical reference, both as illustrator and editor. He is currently in demand for privately commissioned paintings, some of which—particularly the Spoils of War series—are featured in this book.

So often, the problem with imagination is finding an outlet for it, and over the years Zack/Oliver Frey has let his flow onto paper and screen to the great enjoyment of thousands and thousands of fans.

Covers, Adverts, P

Over the years Zack has been called on to produce a plethora of illustrations to sell magazines and books, promote venues, and publicize events. These pictures offer a lively glimpse of the changing gay scene from the 70s to the late 90s.

208 *Heaven Gym Poster*
209 *Christmas Present*
210 *Disco Dancers #1 (Heaven)*
211 *Gay Way Catalog Cover*
212 *Gemini Advert*
213 *Disco Dancers #2 (Heaven)*
214 *Heaven Cellar Advert*
215 *After Lunch Magazine Cover*
216 *Louche Elegance*
217 *Wild Dancing*
218 *Roman Games Heaven Poster*
219 *Cock Gladiator*
220 *Fire island Disco Advert*
220 *Oliver's Bar Advert*
221 *Oliver's Army Poster*
222 *Flask Experiment*
223 *1995 Gay London Scene cover*
223 *Felixitations novel cover*
224 *Meatmen #22 line work*
225 *Meatmen #22 finished cover*
226 *Meatmen #24 rough and line work*
227 *Meatman #24 finished cover*
228 *The Meaning of Real Disco*
229 *1993 Paris Gay Guide*
230 *Street Level London Bar Guide*
230 *Mr. Gay Britain Poster*
231 *The Stripper Centerfold Poster*
232 *Spartan Club Advert*
232 *Travel Young Catalog cover*
233 *Satyricon Theater Poster*

The Gym
Poster for a theme night at Heaven Disco. 1980

Christmas Present
Centerfold poster in 14 Days, *a London events guide.* 1990

Gay Way Brochure
Aspirationally, gay men were finally portrayed as potential loving long-term couples. 1981

*Disco Dancers #1
Advertisement for
Heaven Disco. 1996*

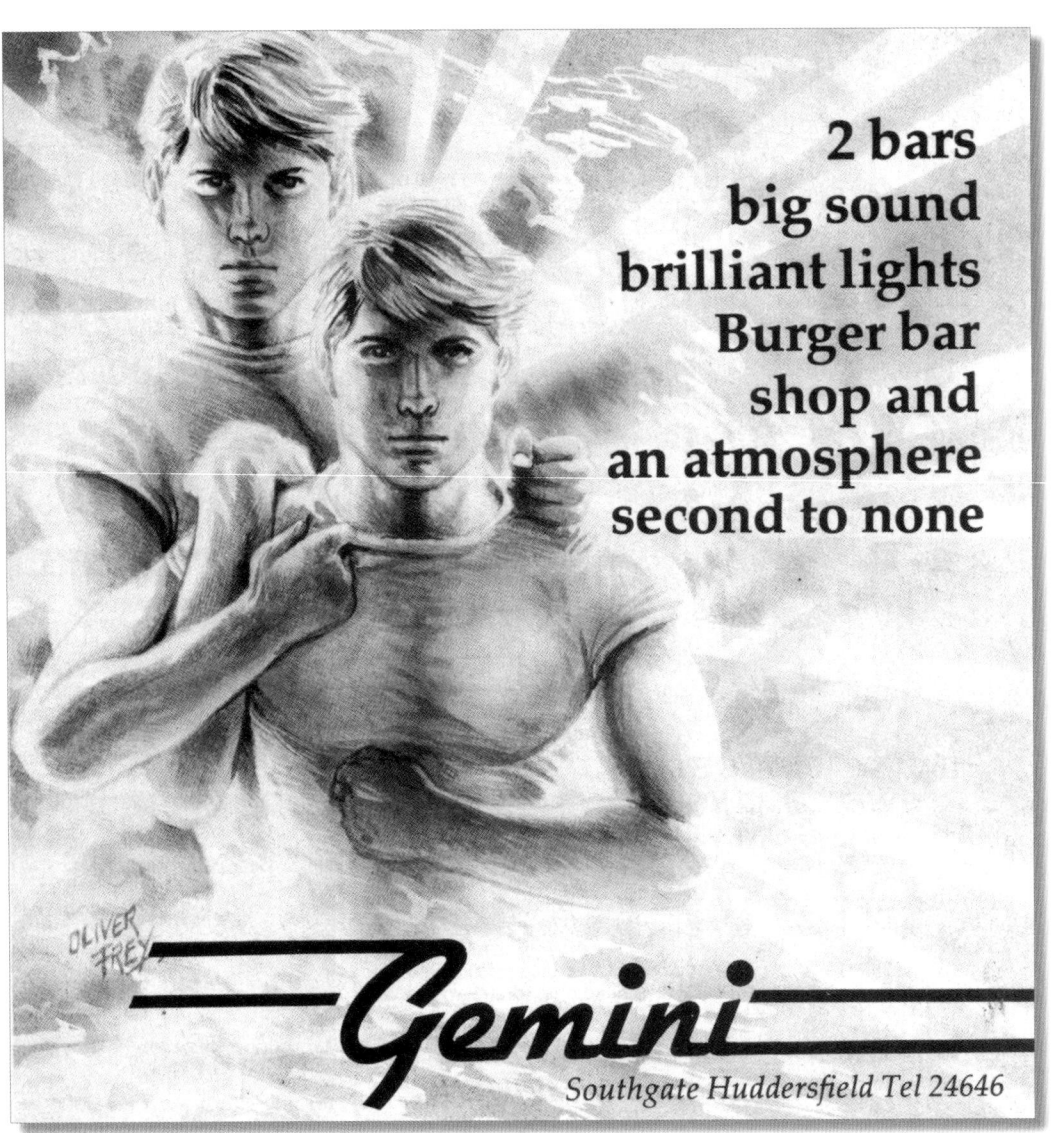

Gemini Twins
1983

Disco Dancers #2
Advertisement for
Heaven Disco. 1996

The Cellar *Advertisement for Heaven Disco's leather club. 1981*

After Lunch
1976

Louche Elegance
Advertisement for
The Hartington Hotel.
1983

Wild Dancing
Advertisement for
Hero's Disco. 1982

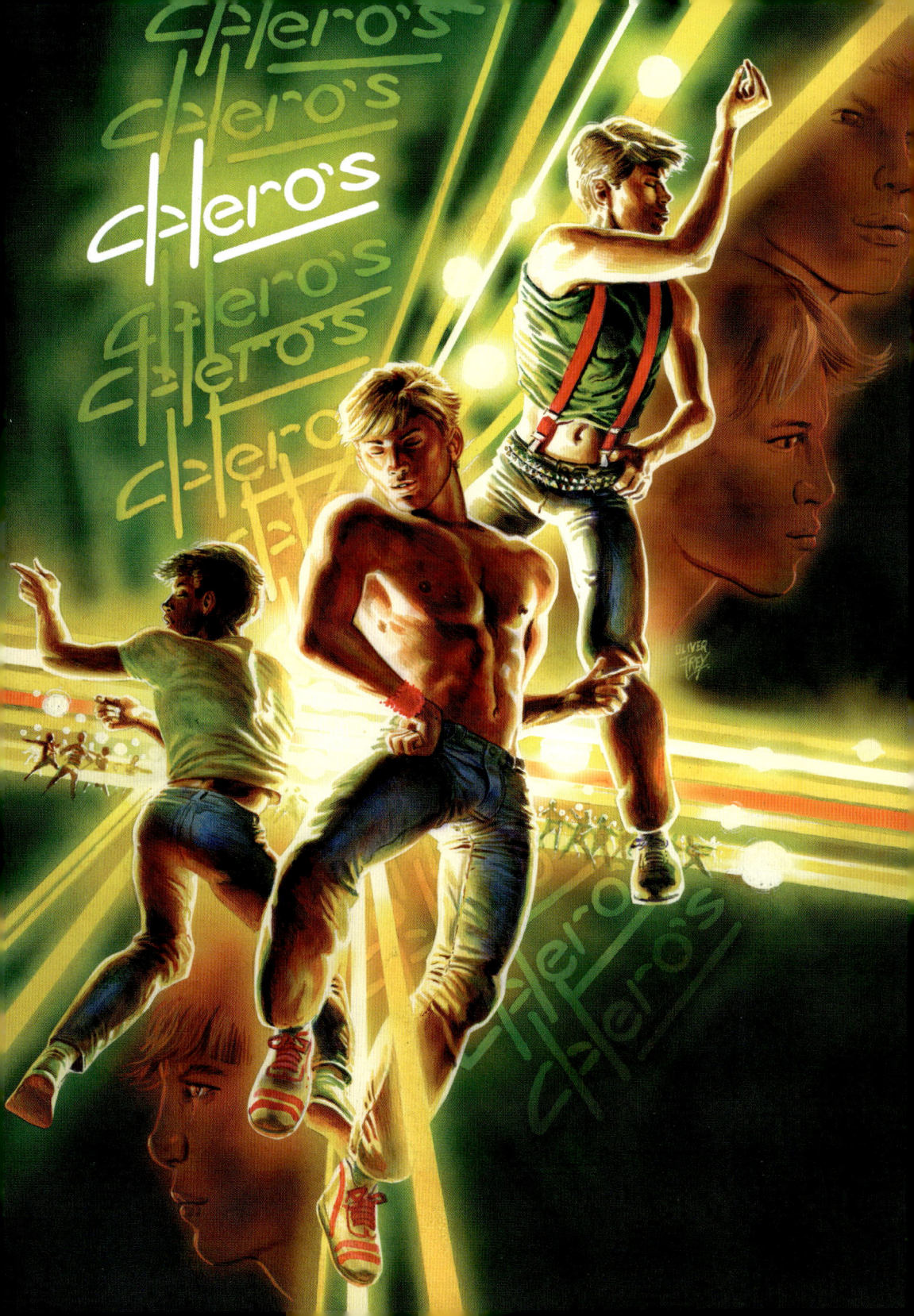

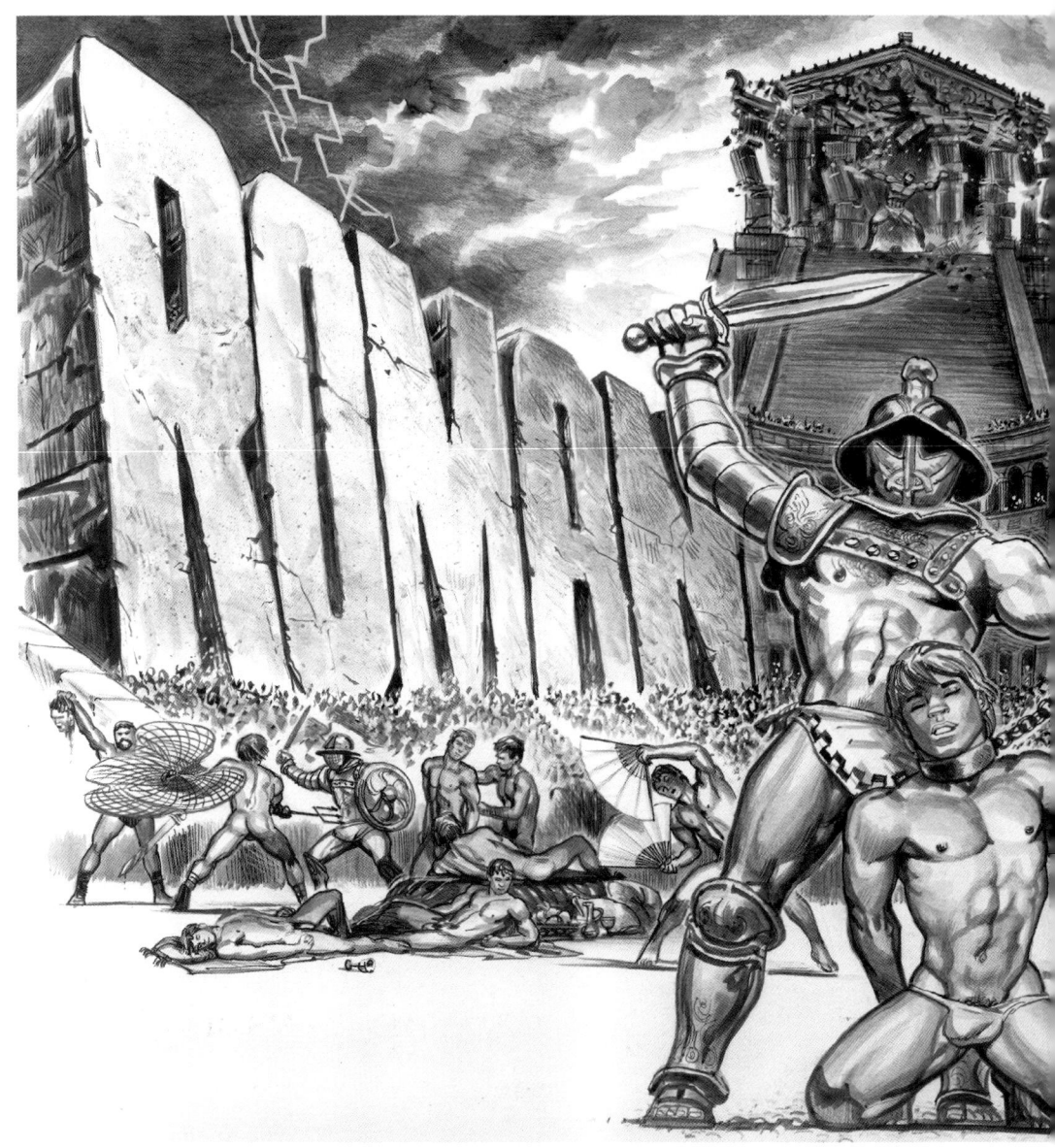

Roman Games
Centerfold in HIM *#33 for the theme night at Heaven Disco. The picture merrily aped the look of epics such as* Ben Hur. *1981*

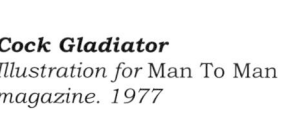

Cock Gladiator
Illustration for Man To Man *magazine. 1977*

Advertisements for Fire Island Disco and Oliver's Club
1993

Oliver's Army
HIM centerfold. Oliver's Army was a play on the hit single by Elvis Costello—as well as the artist's name. 1979

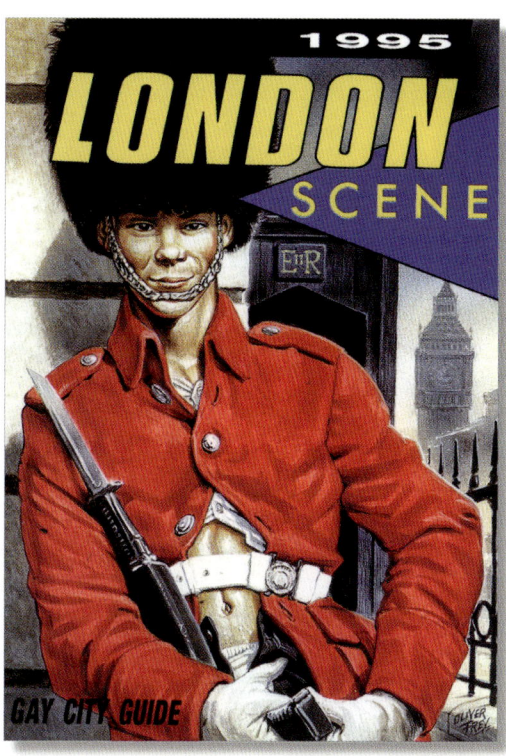

Frey was in demand for gay guide book covers.

Felixitation
Novel cover.
2012

Flask Experiment
AIDS cover for HIM.
It illustrated one
of the first articles
on the subject and
highlighted the
widespread belief
that the illness was
a result of American
health experiments.
A diagonal strap-line
cut across the picture.
1982

Meatmen *comic book cover*
The finished line drawing above and the result after coloring up on computer. 1998

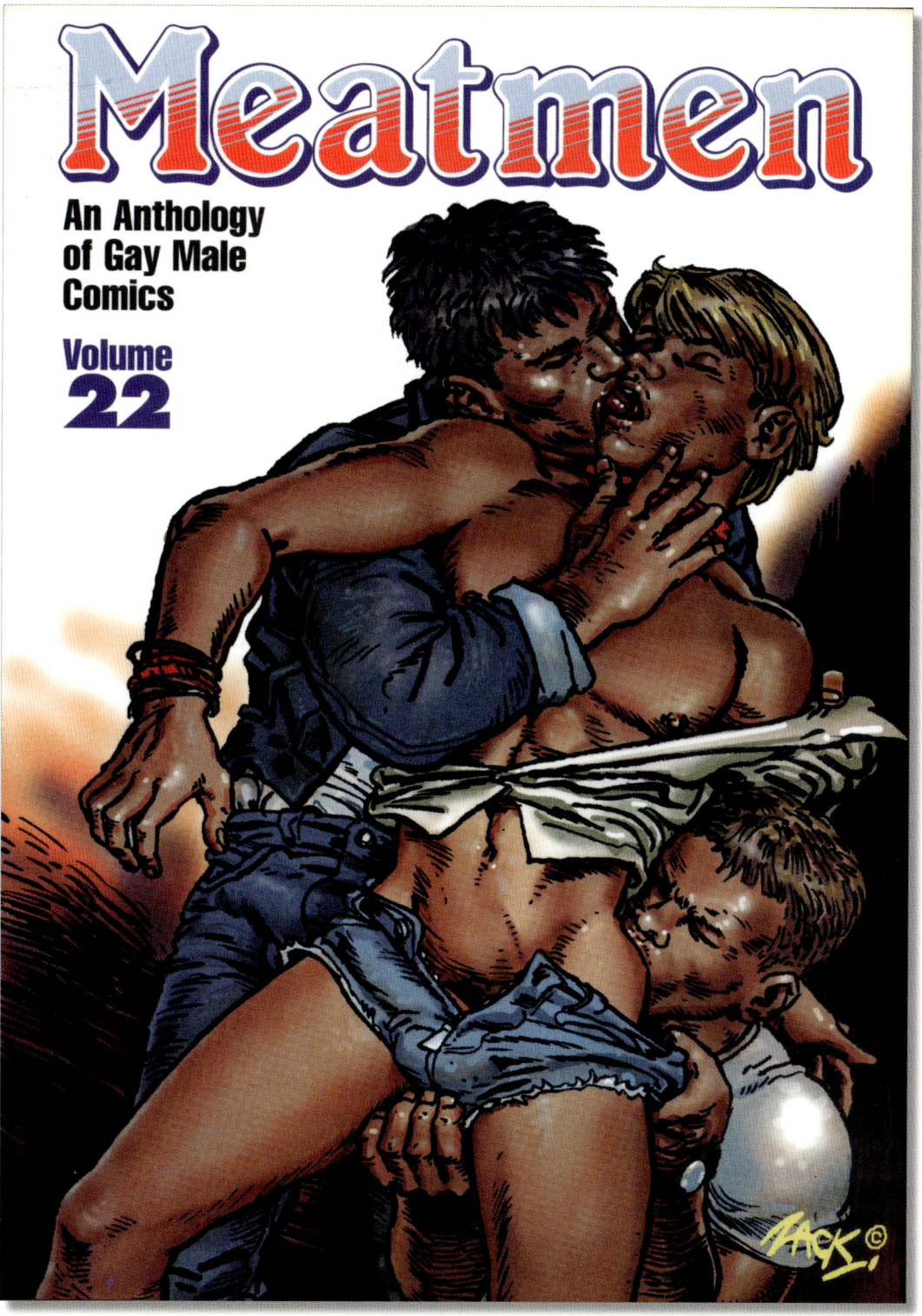

Meatmen **comic book cover** *The pencil rough for publisher approval, left, the finished line drawing, below, and the result after coloring up on computer. 2000*

The Meaning of Real Disco
Advertisement for Heaven Disco. 1982

Street Level Gay Bar Guide
The figure of the boy was painted onto a color photograhic print of Piccadilly Circus. 1978

Mr. Gay Britain
Advertisement for the event held at the Hippodrome Club. Lettering was to appear in the clear area. 1986

The Stripper
Centerfold poster i 14 Days, a Londor events guide. 199

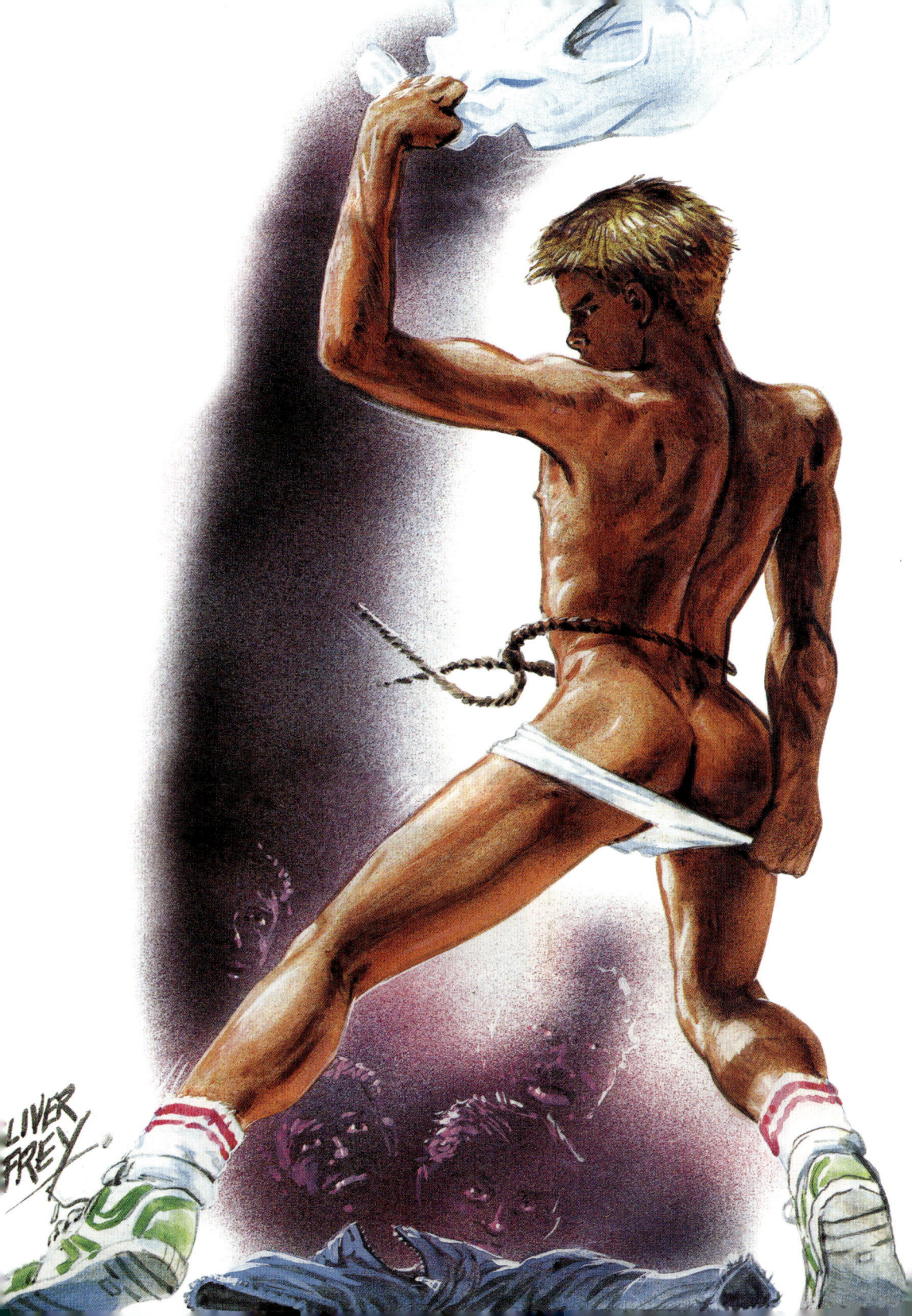

Satyricon
Poster and hoarding for a gay adaption of the story with an American football setting. According to a report in the Evening Standard *paper, the hoarding over the Phoenix Theatre in Charing Cross Road, London led one woman traveling on a bus to cover her young daughter's eyes in horror. 1981*

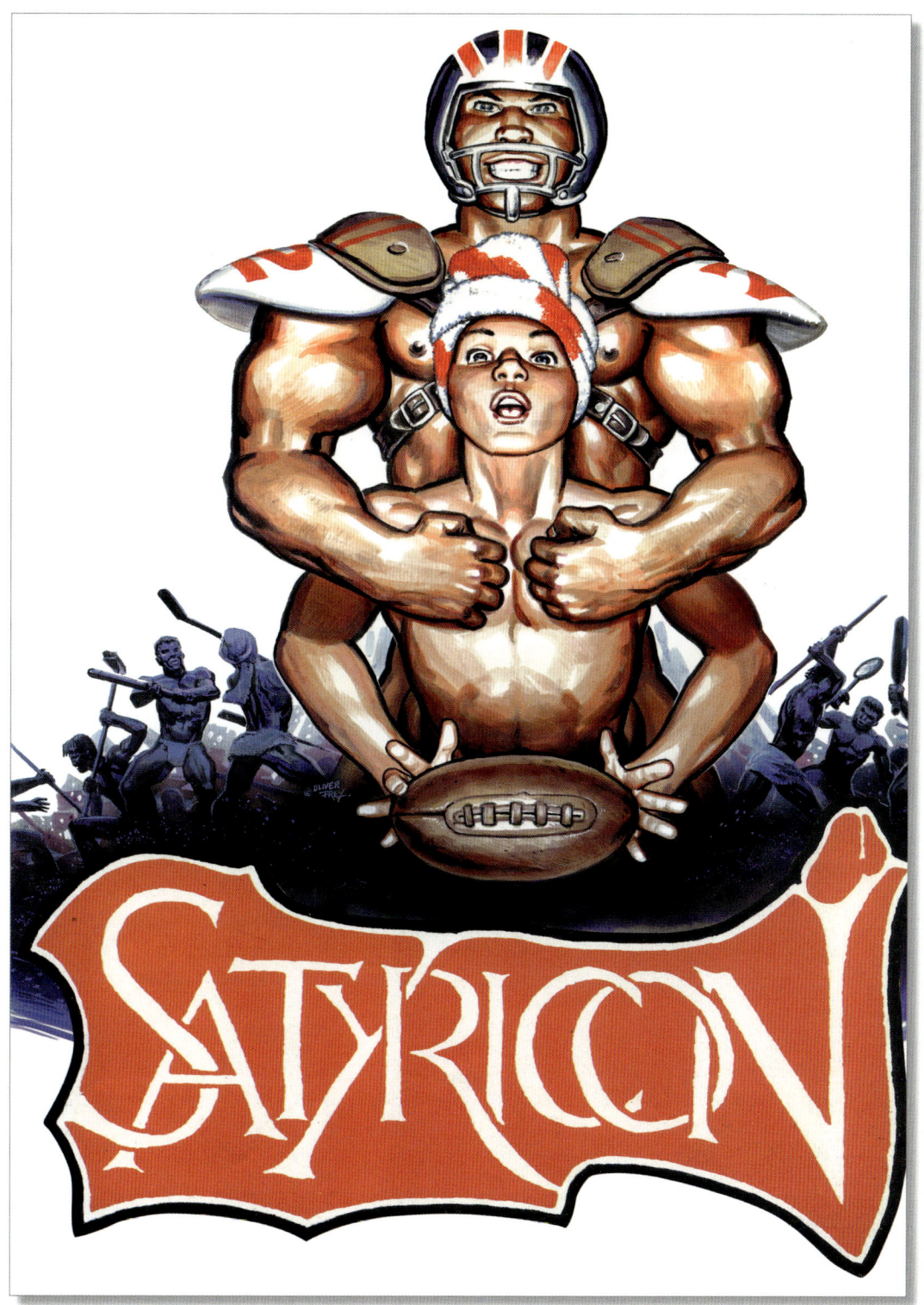

Afterword
by François Peneaud

A Bellamy double page for Heros The Spartan

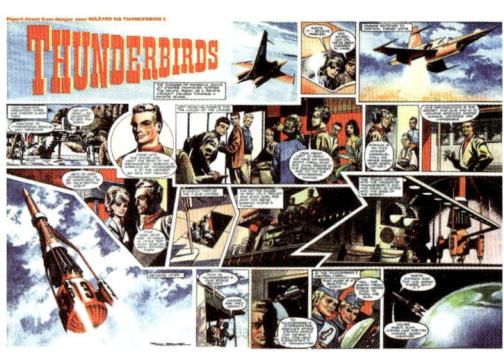

A Bellamy double page for The Thunderbirds

A Frey double page for one of the early Rogue *stories.*

Artists who've done erotic work, especially gay erotic work, are often not considered part of the wider conversation between illustrators and cartoonists, as if erotic work happened in a cultural vacuum. If there's one gay erotic artist for whom that is not true, it's definitely Oliver Frey, or "Zack," as he signed some of his gay work.

I remember first seeing Frey's art in an issue of *Meatmen*, more than a decade ago. I immediately thought he had something more than a lot of his colleagues: not only because of the level of craftsmanship (I had no idea he was a professional illustrator, whereas most *Meatmen* contributors were gifted amateurs), but mainly because his strips were good comics, with an obvious care for the storytelling side of the work. In fact, when a few years ago I began seeing reprints of Frank Hampson, and especially of Frank Bellamy's work (two British mainstream artists of the 50s and 60s whose run on *Dan Dare* or *Thunderbirds* are now considered classic), I realized Oliver Frey had to know these works. As you have read in the words of his partner Roger Kean, I was not wrong.

Of course, Frey is not the only gay artist influenced by comics. See for example Patrick Fillion, who comes from the tradition of superhero comics, Joe Phillips, who's done work for DC and Marvel, or Tom Bouden, who's a direct descendant of Hergé and the Ligne Claire artists. But Frey comes from a different tradition, both in terms of storytelling and of coloring, a

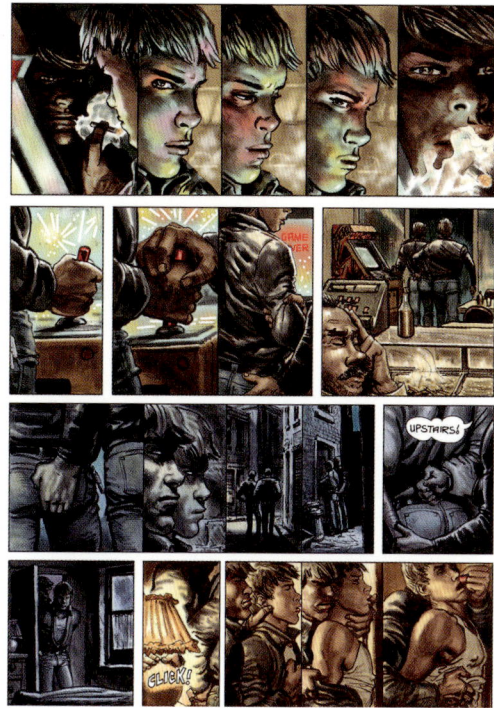

Many of Frey's pages feel more like you're watching moving images than reading static panels. Look at the slight changes in the boy's face as he notices Rogue watching him. Of course, Frey's colors are also put to work, as you can see in the night panels which lead to Rogue and the boy entering Rogue's apartment.

tradition which could have put him on the same path as David Lloyd (*V For Vendetta*), a worthy heir to Hampson and Bellamy.

The strength of Frey's storytelling is in full display in the three comic strips collections published by Bruno Gmünder over the last two years (*Bike Boy*, *Hot For Boys* and *Bike Boy Rides Again*). I won't repeat here what I've already written in various reviews for my website. I'll only say that if you like comics for the way an artist can draw the reader's eye through the page, playing with the confined space he has to contend with, these erotic comics won't please you only for the hot, male flesh content.

In this art book, illustrations, both black & white and in color, take center stage. It seems to me that Oliver Frey's colors are as distinctive as the drawing style itself. This tradition of color comes again from British comics, and has as much to do with the artists' aesthetics as with available means of reproduction: compare a page of 50s Dan Dare from *Eagle* magazine with DC or Marvel comics of the time, and you'll see how limited by the offset printing process US artists were, while Hampson or, later, Bellamy could count on rotogravure to create fully-colored worlds.

As for Oliver Frey, I'd say without trying to generalize too much (and without being an art expert in any way) that his frequent use of monochrome adds an expressionist quality that complements the realism of the line art. After all, color is often about feelings, while the line art is about representation of the real world. The finely-tuned play of light, especially on the bodies of the characters, is also noteworthy. Using a monochromatic ambiance could lead to a dull illustration, but these slivers of light really spice up the art by offering the eye something to hold on to.

The black and white illustrations you have seen in this book are mostly done with the same principles, with gray shading used in lieu of color. The few examples of simply line art are very interesting: take for instance the cover for **Meatmen 22** (→ *Meatmen 22* pages 224, 225). The line art and the colored version are almost two different illustrations, each offering something different to the reader. The colored version might be glossier, but the line art feels more

235

One of the black and white illustrations from the novel Boys of Vice City.

The Street

OLIVER FREY

YOUNG GARETH, NEW TO LONDON AND PENNILESS, DECIDES THAT BEING PICKED UP WILL PROVIDE A BED FOR THE NIGHT...

—BUT GARETH IS STILL A VIRGIN, AND SCARED....

I-I CAN'T GO THROUGH WITH THIS!

WHILE HIS WOULD BE TRICK IS SMACKING HIS LIPS...

A FEW MORE MINUTES AND THE KID WILL BE TWENTY-ONE —AND...

I'LL WHISK HIM HOME AND IT'LL BE NOOKIES ALL THROUGH THE NIGHT!

SLURP!

—ALL MINE! ROGUE CLOCKS UP ANOTHER CONQUEST!

—BUT NEVER COUNT YOUR CHICKENS BEFORE THEY'RE... LAYED!

WELL, GARETH HAPPY B-UH!?

HE'S GONE... CHICKENED OUT!

HUMP! NO KID GETS AWAY FROM ME!

PARADISE IS PACKED...

HE WON'T HAVE LEFT—NOWHERE TO GO...

MAYBE HE'S LOOKING FOR SOME OTHER GUY...

A GENTLE SUGAR DADDY

OR ROUGH TRADE...

THEN—

AH! THERE HE IS—!

WON'T LET CUTIE PIE WRIGGLE OUT NOW!

immediate, maybe because Frey still draws on paper before transferring the drawing to the computer for coloring.

If you like expressive black and white art, I can only recommend that you read the erotic novel *Boys of Vice City*, written by Roger Kean and illustrated by Frey himself. Published over 30 years ago and recently reprinted by Bruno Gmünder, this book includes a large number of ink illustrations, some from the first version and some new, in a style that's closer to late 19th/early 20th century illustrations then found in every magazine and books—though Frey's are far hotter. Another example of Oliver Frey's links to the history of art in general.

A comic strip in black and white also has an important link to gay history, but this time, as an influence: drawn in the early 80s for a British magazine that later became *Gay Times*, *The Street* was a non-explicit strip following the lives of young gay men in the big city. As you can see in the pages shown here, the storytelling was as tight and dense as anything Frey has ever done in gay comics, with the big difference that the focus was not on explicit sex but on the daily lives of the characters, some struggling with their gayness, some only looking for a good time. It even includes a remarkably restrained Rogue (from *Hot For Boys*), who gets to show off his mind instead of his buff body. Unfortunately canceled too soon, this strip could have become as significant as Howard Cruse's *Wendel* in its realistic depiction of the lives of gay men in the 80s. If all that reminds you of Russell T. Davies's TV series *Queer As Folk*, that's not a coincidence, since the man responsible for relaunching a gay-friendly *Doctor Who* has stated his having been impressed by *The Street* when he was young. Which means there's a direct line from *Dan Dare* to *Doctor Who*, and it goes right through

Oliver Frey's gay stories. See what I mean by a conversation between gay artists and the wider artistic continuum?

The Street remains an exception in Frey's career, since his gay-themed work was almost always erotic or explicit. On the other hand, his non-gay work is also full of cute guys, as can be seen in the 2006 book *The Fantasy Art of Oliver Frey*, written by Roger Kean and published by Thalamus Publishing (more about that period of his work in the following biography). Some of his fantasy work is presented in this art book, including a favorite of the artist, the beautiful *Snake Warrior* (page 70), which couldn't contain more phallic symbols if it tried. As much as I respect the cartoonist in Frey, I have to say *Snake Warrior* is proof of his talent to build a single picture that's striking for its strength and apparent simplicity: the horizontal lines made by the sword, the boy's arm and the flame, added to the vertical ones (the carved torch, the boy's body and the small tree—sculpture?—at the bottom right of the painting), ensure the solidity of the composition, while the curved snake and the slanted arm break the monotony of what could have looked like a Roman town's map. I could go on and on about the symbolism in this painting, but I'll only say that *Snake Warrior* is a wonderful painting that's as intellectually pleasing as it is sensual—I'd be hypocritical if I claimed I only enjoyed the verticality of the boy's body.

In fact, this boy warrior could be seen as the embodiment of the kind of boys and men you'll find in Frey's work: boys who are fit and lean, men who remain youthful while being buffer. Everywhere we turn, we find slightly upturned noses, square jaws and little or no body hair. Whether they ride motorbikes, roam

A direct line from Dan Dare to Doctor Who—A Dalek takes its prey: drawing done by Frey for producer Russell T. Davies when he resurrected the famous TV science-fiction series.

Since Frey likes drawing dominant/dominated situations, it's no wonder historical settings are often present in his work: what better pretext for such scenarios than an all-male version of Vikings pillaging a village or what might be Frey's reworking of the Romans abducting Sabine boys instead of women? Violence has often been an excuse for classical painters to show some nudity, and here too, Oliver Frey follows an honored tradition in his own ramped-up way.

Though I admire Oliver Frey's illustrations for the sheer energy they radiate, I consider him to be more a storyteller than an illustrator or a painter. Whether done for a preexisting text or coming directly from Frey's fertile brain, even the seemingly simplest illustration in this book feels like part of a story, through movement, details or setting. The best thing is that, instead of making the readers feel like mere voyeurs, Frey's work is generous enough to be an invitation to create our own stories, to heat up our own fantasies. Oliver Frey's art might be very sexual, but it's also and more importantly open to the whole wide world of history and imagination.

the backstreets of London or partake in Roman orgies, Frey's characters all share characteristics that differentiate them from Tom of Finland's uniformed men or Joe Phillips's boys-next-door.

Beyond the physical types of the characters, another theme quickly emerges: pairings of boys and men are ubiquitous, when the two artists I mentioned usually teamed up guys closer in build and age. Power plays are also at the heart of Oliver Frey's illustrations and comic book works, but sentiments sometimes balance that—or ruin it, depending on your own tastes. I must admit I have a preference for the strips where the older/younger or slave/master relationships are leavened by humor or a sense of the absurd, but I'm sure other readers will enjoy the earnestness and unadulterated eroticism of the more hardcore illustrations.

François Peneaud is a teacher and occasional translator who lives in the South West of France with his partner. He runs the Gay Comics List website and reads too many comics:
http://gaycomicslist.free.fr

239

© 2012-2013 Bruno Gmünder Verlag GmbH
Kleiststraße 23-26, D-10787 Berlin
Phone: +49 30 61 50 03-0
Fax: +49 30 61 50 03-20
info@brunogmuender.com

Editor-in-Chief: Mischa Gawronski
Art Director: Steffen Kawelke
Editorial Coordination: Simeon Morales
Pre Press & Print Management: Zwei G Consult

All artwork © 2012-2013 Oliver Frey
zack-art.com
Afterword © 2012-2013 François Peneaud
Biography © 2012-2013 Roger Kean

All rights reserved. No part of this publication may
be reproduced, stored in a retrieval system, or
transmitted in any form or by any means, electro-
nically or otherwise, without prior consent of the
publisher. All models are 18 years of age or older.

Printed in South Korea

ISBN: 978-3-86787-617-9

Check out all of our books:
www.brunogmuender.com